# WINNER'S MINUTE
## With Mac Hammond

## 365-DAY DEVOTIONAL

Winner's Minute 365-Day Devotional

ISBN 978-1-57399-580-1 © 2020 by Mac Hammond

Published by Mac Hammond Ministries

PO Box 29469 • Minneapolis, MN 55429

Photography Provided By:

Rob Schrader, Bailey Gullo, Bryan Flanagan, Eastman Childs,

Baltimore Medina, Porter Ellenburg, Donny Jiang,  Brandon Cormier,

Weston MacKinnon, Samantha Gades Dobz, and Josh Hild

For nearly twenty years, my family and I have had the privilege of attending Living Word Christian Center. It's been an honor studying under Mac Hammond. Pastor Mac Hammond has always been a visionary leader who seeks new and creative ways to influence people and expand the kingdom of God. When the idea for the Winner's Minute was introduced, my wife and I were truly inspired. *The Winner's Minute* has been able to introduce principles that help people live in victory on a daily basis. I understand the power of these principles as my family and I have benefited greatly from them. The advancements we have experienced personally by his lessons have materialized in our spiritual growth, self-image, relationship growth, and the profitability of our traditional business.

This devotional will take these principles and help them come alive for you as well. Life circumstances will always be changing, but principles that come from the inherent Word of God will never change and can never be stopped. If you have a desire for a deeper relationship with Jesus, as well as a desire to also know the principles of the Kingdom of God, this devotional is your answer.

Matt Grotewald | Leadership Speaker

JANUARY

# Write Down Your Vision

Around 600 B.C., the Hebrew prophet Habakkuk wrote down some advice that could be the key to making this year the best year you've ever had. The prophet wrote an important mandate, inspired by God Himself: "Record the vision and inscribe it on tablets, that the one who reads it may run." He's talking about writing down your goals so you will know the direction in which to run. It was God, not the motivational gurus, who came up with the idea of goal setting as a key to success. Let God give you a vision for the year, write it down, and then go for it.

## Do you have the courage to take Habakkuk's advice?

*And the Lord answered me, and said, Write the vision, and make it plain upon tables, that he may run that readeth it.* (Habakkuk 2:2 KJV)

## 2 Dream Big

Vince Lombardi once stated, "Life's battles don't always go to the stronger or faster man. But sooner or later, the man who wins is the man who thinks he can." We very often place limitations on ourselves. We know our strengths and weaknesses better than anyone else, and we often live our lives accordingly. But I have news for you today. God has a purpose and plan for you that will blow your mind. The Bible says in 1 Corinthians 2:9 that "Eye hath not seen, nor ear heard, neither have entered into the heart of man, the things which God hath prepared for them that love him." I encourage you to dream big because you can't "out dream" God.

Have you allowed God to paint a bold dream on the canvas of your heart?

Now to Him Who, by (in consequence of) the [action of His] power that is at work within us, is able to [carry out His purpose and] do superabundantly, far over and above all that we [dare] ask or think [infinitely beyond our highest prayers, desires, thoughts, hopes, or dreams]— (Ephesians 3:20 Amp.)

# 3 Count the Cost

It's a good thing to have a goal. It's even better if you have a powerful inner drive to achieve it. Without a workable plan, your goal and passion will benefit you very little. Many people are so busy coping with the urgent demands of the present that they tend to let the future take care of itself. We can be so busy putting out fires that we fail to do the planning that would prevent those fires in the first place. In the New Testament, Jesus strongly encourages planning and "counting the cost" when it comes to launching a new venture.

## Do you have a credible plan for achieving your goals?

*For which of you, intending to build a tower, sitteth not down first, and counteth the cost, whether he have sufficient to finish it? Lest haply, after he hath laid the foundation, and is not able to finish it, all that behold it begin to mock him, saying, This man began to build, and was not able to finish.* (Luke 14:28–30 KJV)

#  4 Create Effective Goals

Many people make an effort at setting goals, but few do it effectively. According to the Bible, there are some principles that make your goal setting a powerful tool for achievement. Effective goal setters are willing to discipline themselves, work hard, and sacrifice for delayed gratification. They believe in their God-given gifts and calling. They stay motivated. They form a plan of action, and they have a clear vision of where they're going. I like what a famous German theologian said about goals: "Whatever you can do, or dream you can, begin it; boldness has genius and power in it."

## Have you harnessed the genius and power of lofty goals?

*Wise people think before they act; fools don't—and even brag about their foolishness.* (Proverbs 13:16 NLT)

# 5 Dare to Begin

The reason most plans never succeed—and the reason most goals are never achieved—is because that crucial first step was never taken. Business pioneer Charles Schwab once wrote, "The difference between getting somewhere and nowhere is the courage to make an early start. The fellow who sits still and does just what he is told will never be told to do big things." Likewise, the book of Proverbs repeatedly warns against being like the slothful man who always finds a good excuse for putting off an endeavor. Such a person never achieves great things.

### Is there something you've been putting off that needs to be started?

*Despite their desires, the lazy will come to ruin, for their hands refuse to work.* (Proverbs 21:25 NLT)

# Three Elements of Lasting Change

Do you want to make a lasting change in your behavior? You can if you know the secret of the threefold cord. Behavior has three elements: thoughts, words, and actions. To effect lasting change, you must deal with all three. Changing one element will weaken a bad habit. Changing two will break it. Changing all three will replace the old habit with a new one. Ecclesiastes tells us a threefold cord is not easily broken. So start with the area that's the simplest for you to alter. In some cases that may be your thoughts; in others, it may be your words or actions. No matter where you begin, tackle each element one at a time until you've established that threefold cord. It's a vital step toward starting the New Year with increased self-control.

> Are you willing to pursue lasting change in your life?

*And if one prevail against him, two shall withstand him; and a threefold cord is not quickly broken.* (Ecclesiastes 4:12 KJV)

# Effective Communication

If you want to increase in influence, you're going to have to become a more effective communicator. One true mark of a skilled communicator is knowing what to say, when to say it, and how it should be said. God and His Word are the best resources in the world for developing that level of communication excellence. As your skill in communicating increases, so does your influence on the people you love and those with whom you work. This enables you to impart direction and motivation to your children, your spouse, your coworkers, and your neighbors. I encourage you to ask God to show you how to communicate more effectively.

## Do you communicate effectively?

*There is that speaketh like the piercings of a sword: but the tongue of the wise is health.* (Proverbs 12:18 KJV)

# 8 Willing to Be Visible

An invisible man is not effective in influencing others, because he cannot be seen nor heard. In the same way, if you aren't willing to be visible, you will never affect anyone for God's kingdom. Jesus is our example of this. He spoke from mountain tops and boat bows. He shouted in crowded streets and busy synagogues. He was willing to stand out in a crowd and be a lightning rod for criticism. As Jesus said, a light belongs on a lamp stand, not under a basket.

*Ye are the light of the world. A city that is set on an hill cannot be hid. Neither do men light a candle, and put it under a bushel, but on a candlestick; and it giveth light unto all that are in the house. Let your light so shine before men, that they may see your good works, and glorify your Father which is in heaven.*
(Matthew 5:14–16 KJV)

What can you do to increase your visibility for the Lord?

#  9  What Faith Needs

The old saying is true: "Talk is cheap." William Boetcker put it this way: "The individual activity of one man with backbone will do more than a thousand men with a mere wishbone." When it comes to getting things done, a lot of people talk a good game. People who actually achieve things are much rarer. In the book of James, we're told that faith (or belief) without corresponding action is dead. No one wants to follow someone who is all talk and no results, but people will follow a person of action every time.

> Do people know you as just a talker or as someone who gets things done?

*Even so faith, if it hath not works, is dead, being alone.* (James 2:17 KJV)

# Cultivate Creativity

When you're at your workplace, doing the same job day in and day out, working with the same people, it's easy to get stuck in a box and do your work mindlessly. You can quickly succumb to a trap of conformity about things that were productive at one time, but are now outdated and inefficient. As an employee, creativity is key. Creativity sets you apart in a world of people who do just enough to get by. The organization you work for is growing and changing on a regular basis. You have to change with it. Proverbs 10:4 says, "He becomes poor who works with a slack and idle hand, but the hand of the diligent makes rich." Mindless conformity never contributes to growth; creativity does.

Are you continually looking for the best way to accomplish your job?

*Do you see a man skillful in his work? He will stand before kings; he will not stand before obscure men.* (Proverbs 22:29 ESV)

#  The Alternative to Hurtful Words

When you're in the middle of a heated conversation, it's easy to say whatever comes to your mind. You'll find yourself in less trouble, though, when you decide to keep your mouth shut instead of saying whatever you want. We all need wisdom when dealing with conflict. Sometimes that wisdom is needed to know what to say; other times, it's to help us keep silent. A woman by the name of Dorothy Nevill once stated, "The real art of conversation is not only to say the right thing in the right place but to leave unsaid the wrong thing at the tempting moment." When the only thing you can speak is accusations or hurtful words, your best choice of conversation is silence.

Do you have the discipline to remain silent when you want to say the wrong thing?

*Whoever belittles his neighbor lacks sense, but a man of understanding remains silent.* (Proverbs 11:12 ESV)

# Be a Team Player

If you want to win in the workplace, you will need to be a team player. As Vince Lombardi stated, "The achievements of an organization are the results of the combined effort of each individual." A lot of people have an interest in independently demonstrating how skilled and efficient they are, but working well on your own doesn't make you a quality employee. Teamwork begins when you contribute to the overall effort and produce a corporate result. Lombardi also stated, "People who work together will win, whether it be against complex football defenses or the problems of modern society." I encourage you today to become a team player instead of an independent producer. You—and your workplace—will benefit from it.

## Are you a team player?

*Now I beseech you, brethren, by the name of our Lord Jesus Christ, that ye all speak the same thing, and that there be no divisions among you; but that ye be perfectly joined together in the same mind and in the same judgment.*
(1 Corinthians 1:10 KJV)

# 13 More Important Than Gold

When it comes to exercising influence in the lives of others, there is no more important attribute you can possess than personal integrity. The Bible tells us that integrity made King David a great leader, and a lapse in that integrity nearly cost him his throne. As philanthropist Roger W. Babson once said, "A character standard is far more important than a gold standard. The success of all economic systems is still dependent upon both righteous leaders and righteous people. In the last analysis, our national future depends upon our national character—that is, whether it is spiritually or materially minded." When you speak, people need to know your words and actions will both be honorable.

When it comes to your interactions with others, are your words and actions as good as gold?

*"Better to be poor and honest than to be dishonest and rich."* (Proverbs 28:6 NLT)

## 14 God's Path to Blessing

Think for a moment about the things that make life good. Love, friendship, encouragement, financial increase, promotion on the job, and recognition of achievement: all these things have one thing in common. They come through the channel of relationships. Nearly every form of blessing and increase comes as a direct result of relationships with other people. That's why the quality of your relationships and your skill in cultivating those relationships has a profound impact on your quality of life.

> Are you willing to receive God's blessing through your relationships?

*Two are better than one; because they have a good reward for their labour. For if they fall, the one will lift up his fellow: but woe to him that is alone when he falleth; for he hath not another to help him up. Again, if two lie together, then they have heat: but how can one be warm alone?* (Ecclesiastes 4:9–11 KJV)

#  Duplicate Yourself

How many leaders are confident enough to encourage their subordinates to surpass them? Jesus was just such a leader. He once told His disciples, "Greater things than I have done, you shall do" (John 14:12). The goal of Jesus' leadership was to duplicate Himself in those under His care and raise up others who could carry on His mission. Insecure leaders find this impossible, but wise leaders follow this pattern.

> Are you secure enough in your place to duplicate yourself?

*Verily, verily, I say unto you, He that believeth on me, the works that I do shall he do also; and greater works than these shall he do; because I go unto my Father.* (John 14:12 KJV)

## 16 What Do You Expect?

Parents, if you want your children to succeed, expect that they will—even if you don't see signs of success right away. Studies show that children with the IQ of a genius will not live up to their full potential if their parents expect them to fail in life. Employers, this is true for you as well. Your greatest motivational tool as a leader is to genuinely expect your employees to "hang the moon." Educator Kingman Brewster Jr. put it this way: "There is no greater challenge than to have someone relying upon you; no greater satisfaction than to vindicate his expectation." So today I encourage you to expect the best out of those around you and especially out of anyone under your authority.

Do you expect those underneath your authority to succeed in life?

*For surely there is an end; and thine expectation shall not be cut off.*
(Proverbs 23:18 KJV)

# People First, Technology Second

Over the past few years, technology has increased the ways we can communicate with each other, but it hasn't necessarily increased the effectiveness of our communication. Should we add Instagram? Facebook and Twitter, email and texting—all of these forms of communication can be good things, but never let them become your sole source of communication. Nothing can replace the personal connection achieved through a face-to-face conversation. Technology is a great way to pass along facts; but it cannot convey emotion, and it can easily be misconstrued. When you have something important to say to someone, take the time to tell him in person.

Who runs your relationships: you or technology?

*Therefore all things whatsoever ye would that men should do to you, do ye even so to them: for this is the law and the prophets.* (Matthew 7:12 KJV)

# 18 Kindness Is Key

People often assume that the person most impacted by kindness is the one who receives it, but that's not necessarily true. As Booker T. Washington once said, "If you want to lift yourself up, lift up someone else." Kindness is not a value that should be conditional on circumstances, rather it should be given unconditionally to everyone. Frenchman Joseph Joubert said it this way: "Kindness is loving people more than they deserve." Unconditional kindness is the fruit of a life lived well, but it's not something that comes naturally. It is something we work toward each day. If you want to win in your relationships, remember that kindness is key.

## Who can you be kind to today?

*And be ye kind one to another, tenderhearted, forgiving one another, even as God for Christ's sake hath forgiven you.* (Ephesians 4:32 KJV)

# Practice Godly Communication

News of corruption in politics is commonplace, but did you know your own communication can be corrupt? You may consider yourself a smooth talker. Maybe you can banter with the best of them. Whatever it may be, to be truly successful, you need to avoid something the Bible calls "corrupt communication." It's conversation that produces a negative result, such as gossip, mean-spirited criticism, or complaining. The Bible wisely warns us to steer clear of such communication. Say only what will help and encourage others. Keep your conversations free of coarseness, jealousy, and envy. Avoid corrupt communication, and the results will surprise you. You will wield more favor and influence than you ever thought possible.

## What can you do to ensure that corrupt communication remains far from you?

*Let no corrupt communication proceed out of your mouth, but that which is good to the use of edifying, that it may minister grace unto the hearers.*
(Ephesians 4:29 KJV)

## Use the Paraphrase

Studies have found that people commonly listen to the first two sentences of a conversation, and then miss a large portion of what is being said next because they start mentally putting together their own response. The art of being a good hearer involves taking time to listen to what the other person is saying. One way you can ensure you do that is by using the paraphrase, something Jesus used a lot on this earth. Take what the other person said and run it back to him in different phrasing to make sure you understand what he is trying to convey. That gives that person an opportunity to correct you if you are wrong, allows enough time to pass so emotional dust can settle, and gives you the chance to form a response. The paraphrase will help you become a better listener.

Will you put aside your desire to talk so you can listen properly to other people?

*If one gives an answer before he hears, it is his folly and shame.*
(Proverbs 18:13 ESV)

# Become a Person of Action

"Don't just stand there. Do something." When you have responsibility, it's all too easy to become frozen in indecision. Some have called it "the paralysis of analysis." Jesus never suffered from this malady; He was a man of action. He spoke when words were necessary. He intervened when intervention was needed. With purpose and focus, He did what needed to be done. I challenge you to follow in His footsteps: become a person of action.

Where have you become paralyzed in life and what action can you take to break free and move forward?

*I can already hear one of you agreeing by saying, "Sounds good. You take care of the faith department, I'll handle the works department." Not so fast. You can no more show me your works apart from your faith than I can show you my faith apart from my works. Faith and works, works and faith, fit together hand in glove.* (James 2:18 Msg.)

# 22 Include Family

When some managers hire an individual, they fail to realize they have actually hired that person's entire family. They forget that his or her best performance will only be forthcoming when there are no distracting problems at home. In fact, the first miracle Jesus ever performed was done at a wedding; it was just one of many examples of how Jesus did things for the family members of His followers. Jesus always showed that He cared about the loved ones of those close to Him. What a powerful and valuable lesson.

Are you building loyalty and productivity by showing concern for your employees' families?

*Let each of you look not only to his own interests, but also to the interests of others.* (Philippians 2:4 ESV)

**23** Prepare Adequately

Whether you're laying the foundation for a career, launching a product, or making a presentation, there is no substitute for preparation. Jesus taught us powerfully about preparation, both in His example and in His words. Many of the parables He used admonish us to be well prepared. Jesus personally prepared for thirty years before executing His plan. We may not have thirty years to prepare, but the principle remains the same. Preparation prepares us properly for the future.

Are you preparing adequately or trying to fly by the seat of your pants?

*Go to the ant, thou sluggard; consider her ways, and be wise: which having no guide, overseer, or ruler, provideth her meat in the summer, and gathereth her food in the harvest.* (Proverbs 6:6–8 KJV)

## 24 What Do You Desire?

The Bible makes it clear that desire is an important element in our achievements. As one writer put it, "The strength of your desire determines the distance you're likely to travel." Healthy desire for a goal or objective creates the impetus to overcome the obstacles that lie in your path. If you look up "desire" in your thesaurus, you'll find synonyms like hunger, longing, and yearning. People with desire work harder, are more focused on their goals, and achieve more. Why? Their hunger propels them forward when others fall by the wayside. In Psalm 37:4 we read, "Delight yourself in the Lord and he will give you the desires of your heart." Purpose to be a person who delights in God, and you'll soon find yourself obtaining your heart's desire.

## What desires dominate your life the most?

*Delight thyself also in the Lord; and he shall give thee the desires of thine heart.*
(Psalm 37:4 KJV)

# Patient Listening

Are you a patient listener? Given the fact that you can think four times faster than someone can talk, you're going to have to be if you want to master leadership through listening. There are striking parallels between keys to effective listening and truths found in the Bible. One of those keys is concentrated patience. When your thoughts race ahead of a speaker's words, you can become detached and miss important information. The Bible says that patience is better than pride. Don't jump to conclusions. Be a patient and focused listener and your leadership effectiveness will grow.

Are you truly listening to what others have to say?

*Better is the end of a thing than the beginning thereof: and the patient in spirit is better than the proud in spirit.* (Ecclesiastes 7:8 KJV)

# 26 What Are You Thinking?

When people hear what the Bible has to say about changing your life by changing your thought patterns, they sometimes remark that it sounds like "positive thinking." In reality, much of what has been written about positive thinking sounds like the Bible. Proverbs says, "As a man thinks in his heart, so is he." In Romans chapter 12, Paul tells us we can be transformed by the renewing of our minds. Paul was saying that changing the way you think will change who you are and how you behave.

## How has your thinking been?

*And be not conformed to this world: but be ye transformed by the renewing of your mind, that ye may prove what is that good, and acceptable, and perfect, will of God.* (Romans 12:2 KJV)

# 27 What Others Want

Imagine for a moment that a husband buys his wife a fishing pole because he wants her to fish with him. Or a math teacher buys his son a calculator because he wants his son to love math as much he does. Both the husband and the teacher may be disappointed when their gifts aren't received well because the wife hates fishing and the son prefers English. The gifts were a nice idea, but they were given on the basis of what the giver wanted, not what the receiver liked. If you want to bless someone, bless them on the basis of what they would like, not on what you want them to have. This is one way you can put other people's needs in front of your own—and consistently win in relationships.

> Whose ideas are more important: yours or someone else's?

*Be kindly affectioned one to another with brotherly love; in honour preferring one another;* (Romans 12:10 KJV)

Influence vs. Control

If you're skillful at building strong relationships, you know you can't control others, but you can influence them. In Deuteronomy 30:19, God tells His people, "I have set before you life and death, blessing and cursing: therefore choose life." God has placed in each of us a will and freedom to choose; because of that, God will not override a person's free will. Keep that in mind in your dealings with others. To have healthy relationships, you cannot control others. Strong relationships are based on influence, not control. It's an important trait of a winning relationship builder.

*You're here to be light, bringing out the God-colors in the world. God is not a secret to be kept. We're going public with this, as public as a city on a hill. If I make you light-bearers, you don't think I'm going to hide you under a bucket, do you? I'm putting you on a light stand. Now that I've put you there on a hilltop, on a light stand—shine!* (Matthew 5:14–16 Msg.)

Are you influencing those around you or trying to control them?

Image • Eastman Childs

# Consistency Is Key

Have you ever found yourself using the phrase, "Just do it because I'm the boss"? If you have, you probably realized it doesn't work that well. People will respond out of intimidation, but if given the opportunity, they will get out from under your leadership as soon as they can. Author William Arthur Ward stated, "Leadership is based on inspiration, not domination; on cooperation, not intimidation." If you truly want to influence the people around you, you need to become a leader people want to follow. One way you can do that is by remaining consistent. When you are consistent in your attitude, words, and deeds, people know what they can expect from you. That consistency builds trust in you as a leader and brings you one step closer to being a leader people want to follow.

## Are you a consistent leader?

*Therefore, my beloved brethren, be ye stedfast, unmoveable, always abounding in the work of the Lord, forasmuch as ye know that your labour is not in vain in the Lord.* (1 Corinthians 15:58 KJV)

# 30  Be Generous

We've all heard the saying, "What goes around comes around." It's an unchangeable principle in God's universe. Jesus affirmed this truth when He said, "Give, and it shall be given unto you; good measure, pressed down, and shaken together, and running over." Would you like to be prosperous and live a refreshed life? Decide today to be a generous person.

## Is generosity an important quality in your life?

*The generous will prosper; those who refresh others will themselves be refreshed.* (Proverbs 11:25 NLT)

#  Graceful Waiting

No one likes to wait. In this fast-food society, everyone expects instantaneous results. Unfortunately, Christians aren't immune to this mentality. All too often, they become disillusioned if their prayers aren't answered right away. The truth is, they could shorten their waiting period if they simply learned to wait gracefully. Waiting on the Lord is a Christian discipline that has been lost to the body of Christ. Too many people become disappointed when their expectation is frustrated and they have to wait longer than they think for their prayers to get met. That's why it's important for us to learn how to wait gracefully before the Lord.

# How are you waiting?

*The Lord is good*

*unto them that wait for him,*

*to the soul that seeketh him.*

(Lamentations 3:25 KJV)

Image • Eastman Childs

Image • Baltimore Medina

FEBRUARY

# 1 Monitor Your Motives

It's not always "what" you do, but "why" you do it. What is your motive? It's healthy to stop and check your motives every so often. It's possible to be doing all the right things for all the wrong reasons. Proverbs 16:2 says, "All the ways of a man are clean in his own sight, but the Lord weighs the motives." James 4:3 says, "You do not have because you do not ask. You ask and do not receive, because you ask with wrong motives." Doing good things with unhealthy motives may work for a time, but will ultimately backfire. Endeavor to keep your motives pure.

## Have you examined your motives recently?

*Even a child is known by his doings, whether his work be pure, and whether it be right.* (Proverbs 20:11 KJV)

## Avoid Gossip

Have you heard the latest office gossip? Every office, corporation, or workplace has it—a steady flow of juicy gossip filled with rumor, conjecture, and wild speculation. But if you want to be happy on the job, you need to avoid this kind of talk. Participating in gossip is tempting but destructive. The Bible is filled with warnings to avoid it. James 4:11 says, "Speak not evil of one another." Proverbs 17:9 says, "He who covers over an offense promotes love, but whoever repeats a matter separates close friends." Refuse to participate in gossip in the workplace, and you'll earn the respect and trust of everyone around you.

Are you willing to stop gossip in its tracks whenever you hear it?

*A talebearer revealeth secrets: but he that is of a faithful spirit concealeth the matter.* (Proverbs 11:13 KJV)

# ③ Step Away From the Cloak of Shame

Any time you feel incapable of moving forward because of something from your past, I encourage you to question that line of thinking. Doubt the doubts that say you are less than enough. Let the story in your mind resound with a new truth: you were created with a purpose and there's a plan on your life for you to fulfill. Max Lucado put it this way: "You are valuable because you exist, not because of what you do or what you have done, but simply because you are." Shame and guilt don't have to shackle your life forever. Let forgiveness cloak your relationships— and then dig into your God-given potential and let your dreams become a reality.

Where have you let shame keep you
from reaching for your dreams?

*Instead of your shame there shall be a double portion; instead of dishonor they shall rejoice in their lot; therefore in their land they shall possess a double portion; they shall have everlasting joy.* (Isaiah 61:7 ESV)

#  FOMO: Get Over it!

Globalization has led to the spread of an interesting phenomenon—something social media enhances and advertisers capitalize on. It's called FOMO—the fear of missing out. An article in Boston magazine stated, "FOMO sufferers report being unable to tear themselves away from their Facebook and Instagram feeds, ironically making it harder to engage in real life. For many, the fear of missing out has become self-fulfilling." If you've dealt with this in any form, I have three words for you: get over it. The grass appears greener in other places because it has been watered better than the grass under your own feet. Invest in your own life by being fully present in what you're doing today.

### Are you focusing on your life or someone else's?

*A sound heart is the life of the flesh: but envy the rottenness of the bones.* (Proverbs 14:30 KJV)

# 5 Luck Doesn't Work

In the minds of more and more Americans, the key to success is not hard work, ingenuity, or resourcefulness. People seem to believe the key to success is luck. According to the Bible, though, there is no such thing as luck. Success is a product of operating by certain principles. Ralph Waldo Emerson concurred. He once wrote: "Shallow men believe in luck and circumstance. Strong men believe in cause and effect." Today millions of Americans are pinning their hopes and dreams for a brighter future on a lottery ticket rather than sweat and creativity. A belief in blind luck is just another false assumption that will keep you from winning in life.

## Have you been leaning on luck instead of working hard toward success?

*...If anyone is not willing to work, let him not eat. For we hear that some among you walk in idleness, not busy at work, but busybodies. Now such persons we command and encourage in the Lord Jesus Christ to do their work quietly and to earn their own living.* (2 Thessalonians 3:10–12 ESV)

#  The Danger of Offense

Offense is harmful to relationships. That's why we must do all we can to keep away from offense. One way we do this is by placing a premium on conflict resolution. When addressing a disagreement, keep in mind the needs of the other person. Don't attempt to solve conflict when one or both of you are exhausted. If you're too tired to think well, you could easily revert to protecting yourself at the cost of hurting the other person. If emotions are raging, irrational thinking will rule. If you want to avoid offending or being offended, solve a situation when neither of you are exhausted, emotions have calmed, and you both can think clearly.

> Are you keeping offense as far from your relationships as you can?

*That we henceforth be no more children, tossed to and fro, and carried about with every wind of doctrine, by the sleight of men, and cunning craftiness, whereby they lie in wait to deceive; but speaking the truth in love, may grow up into him in all things, which is the head, even Christ.* (Ephesians 4:14–15 KJV)

# 7 Criticism Can Benefit You

Nobody likes to be criticized. It's doubly painful when those remarks come from the boss. Nonetheless, people who are consistently happy at work tend to have a common characteristic: they use criticism to their advantage. Instead of getting offended by criticism, they use it as an opportunity to examine and improve themselves. In Proverbs 13:18, the Bible says, "He who ignores instruction comes to poverty and shame, but whoever heeds correction is honored." Respond positively to criticism, and you'll be a long way toward finding happiness on the job.

## How do you handle constructive criticism?

*Give instruction to a wise man, and he will be yet wiser: teach a just man, and he will increase in learning.* (Proverbs 9:9 KJV)

# 8 Wisdom Wins

If you could instantly acquire one characteristic, what would it be? What one personal attribute would make life better and more successful? If you ask a hundred people, some would say, "Intelligence," and others may say, "Charm." Still others might say, "Self-confidence" or "Wit." The Bible provides a different answer to that question in Proverbs 4:7 where we read, "Wisdom is the principal thing." In other words, no matter what it is you want to achieve, it begins with wisdom. Wisdom is more than just knowledge. Knowledge is information. Wisdom is the ability to take that information and make good decisions.

Do you possess the quality of wisdom or have you merely accumulated knowledge?

*If any of you lack wisdom, let him ask of God, that giveth to all men liberally, and upbraideth not; and it shall be given him.* (James 1:5 KJV)

# 9 Say Thanks

Saint Ambrose once said, "No duty is more urgent than that of returning thanks." William James wrote that "The deepest principle in human nature is the craving to be appreciated." There is no doubt about it; people thrive in an environment of appreciation. The Bible has a lot to say about maintaining a thankful heart, both to God and to those whose efforts contribute to your success. Jesus consistently expressed a heart of gratitude. Read His words, and you'll find Him constantly expressing gratitude to God and to those around Him. In business and in life, it is impossible to say thank you too many times or in too many ways.

What creative way can you say thanks to the people in your life today?

*In every thing give thanks: for this is the will of God in Christ Jesus concerning you.* (1 Thessalonians 5:18 KJV)

# The Power of an Idea

We all have those moments where we have an idea about how to do something better. Maybe it's regarding your productivity at work or a new business idea or an educational endeavor. Don't take those ideas for granted. Business speaker Seth Godin put it this way: "Today, not starting is far, far worse than being wrong. If you start, you've got a shot at evolving and adjusting to turn your wrong into a right. But if you don't start, you never get a chance." Not every idea will revolutionize your life, but you won't know unless you try.

Is there an idea you've set aside that God wants to bring to the forefront of your thinking?

And he has filled him with the Spirit of God, with skill, with intelligence, with knowledge, and with all craftsmanship, to devise artistic designs, to work in gold and silver and bronze.
(Exodus 35:3121 ESV)

# The Force of Faith

"All things are possible to those who believe." Those words were spoken by Jesus of Nazareth more than two thousand years ago, and they are just as true today. Faith, belief, or conviction is the reservoir from which we draw power. It provides that extra push that helps us carry on in adversity. More importantly, the very universe was created to respond and change in the face of faith. As President Coolidge once said, "Faith is the great motive power, and no man realizes his full possibilities unless he has the deep conviction that his life is eternally important, and that his work, well done, is part of an unending plan."

Have you harnessed the unlimited power of faith in the achievement of your dreams?

*And without faith it is impossible to please him, for whoever would draw near to God must believe that he exists and that he rewards those who seek him.* (Hebrews 11:6 NIV)

# 12 Season Your Speech

You probably know someone who always seems to say just the right words at the right time. Most people aren't born with that gift. It's cultivated and developed. According to Colossians 4:6, it is something you acquire by adding "grace" and "seasoning" to your speech: "Let your speech always be with grace, seasoned, as it were, with salt, so that you may know how you should respond to each person." Effective, timely, gracious communication gives you the right word for every occasion, and it's an identifying mark of a winner.

## Is your speech seasoned with grace?

*Set a watch, O Lord, before my mouth; keep the door of my lips.* (Psalm 141:3 KJV)

#  Show Others True Love

A proven way to win in your relationships is to show love to the other person. I'm not talking about the romantic love between a husband and a wife. I'm talking about the God kind of love: *agape* love—a love that gives without expecting anything in return. John 3:16 says, "For God so loved the world that He *gave* His one and only begotten Son...." If we want to win in our relationships, we will put others' needs in front of our own. Perhaps that means you hand over the TV remote to your spouse or buy your friend dinner instead of buying yourself a new pair of shoes. Whatever it is, when you show other people that you care more about their needs than your own, you'll win in those relationships every time.

## Are you ready to love your family and friends unconditionally?

*This is my commandment, That ye love one another, as I have loved you. Greater love hath no man than this, that a man lay down his life for his friends.* (John 15:12–13 KJV)

## 14 Redefine Romance

It's amazing how many couples act as though marriage signals the end to romancing your spouse, but that's not true. Romance is the glue that keeps your marriage together. The reason romance disappears after marriage is often because couples stop communicating their love to each other. Husbands and wives, I encourage you to be open about your affection for each other. Say "I love you" when you talk on the phone. Bring each other gifts of appreciation. Spend time with your spouse. Find out what your spouse appreciates and do it as a heartfelt expression of your love. Your marriage will thrive when you learn to continually communicate how much you love each other. Keep romance alive!

If you are married, do you still "date" your spouse and let the romance continue?

*Let your wife be a foundation of blessing for you. Rejoice in the wife of your youth.* (Proverbs 5:18 NLT)

#  The Humility Test

It's been said that the first test of a truly great man is his humility. The prideful and the arrogant are rarely effective at influencing others. That's because very few people allow themselves to be influenced by someone who looks down on them. If we ever want to impact those around us, we will need to have a humble spirit. The Bible repeatedly encourages us not to "think more highly of ourselves than we ought." William Penn echoed this biblical truth when he wrote, "Sense shines with a double luster when it is set in humility. An able and yet humble man is a jewel worth a kingdom."

## How do you score on the humility test?

*The Lord supports the humble, but he brings the wicked down into the dust.*
(Psalm 147:6 NLT)

# 16 Mix Excellence With Integrity

Integrity and excellence go hand in hand. It's been said that integrity is a passion for doing the right thing while excellence comes from a passion for doing things right. Proverbs tells us that those who achieve excellence in their field will stand before kings. Excellence can be defined as the gradual result of consistent improvement. According to historian Will Durant, Aristotle's ideas matched what was written time and again in Proverbs: "Excellence is an art won by training and habituation...we are what we repeatedly do. Excellence, then, is not an act but a habit."

## Is this powerful combination of characteristics active in your life?

*Seest thou a man diligent in his business? he shall stand before kings; he shall not stand before mean men.* (Proverbs 22:29 KJV)

 Delegate

Have you ever been given responsibility for doing something without the corresponding authority to get it done? It's a horrible position in which to be placed. Jesus knew that if He gave His followers responsibility, He must also delegate His authority. If more leaders today understood this leadership secret, much more would be accomplished. Of course, delegating authority involves some risks. And the leader who does so must be secure enough not to need to receive all the credit.

## Have you given someone responsibility without authority?

*And Moses chose able men out of all Israel, and made them heads over the people, rulers of thousands, rulers of hundreds, rulers of fifties, and rulers of tens. And they judged the people at all seasons: the hard causes they brought unto Moses, but every small matter they judged themselves. (Exodus 18:25–26 KJV)*

## 18  Persevere

Dr. Seuss's first children's book was rejected by over twenty-three publishers before being accepted. That one book eventually became over 44 published books with more than 650 million copies sold. Dr. Seuss died knowing his perseverance resulted in entertaining and educating millions of children. Perseverance is all too rare a commodity these days. John D. Rockefeller is quoted as saying, "I do not think there is any other quality so essential to success of any kind as the quality of perseverance. It overcomes almost everything, even nature."

Is the quality of perseverance a reality in your life?

*But ye, brethren, be not weary in well doing.* (2 Thessalonians 3:13 KJV)

February

 # Shielded by Favor

How would you like to find goodwill, acceptance, and consideration everywhere you go? If that sounds good, you're in the market for something the Bible calls "favor." For some people, doors of opportunity always seem to swing open wide. Their relationships tend to be mutual pathways of blessing and help. It's not luck these people are exhibiting; it's favor—and it's something God bestows on those who put themselves in a position to qualify. The fifth Psalm says, "For surely, O Lord, you bless the righteous; you surround them with your favor as with a shield." Imagine carrying an invisible shield of goodwill wherever you go.

## Do you see God's favor at work in your life?

*For you bless the righteous, O Lord; you cover him with favor as with a shield.*
(Psalm 5:12 ESV)

# Rightly Relate to Authority

Think about the people who are in authority over you. It could be a supervisor at work. It could be a parent. It could be some sort of spiritual authority. These represent a special type of relationship—a type God wants to use to bring four very important benefits to bear in your life. Those benefits are instruction, correction, direction, and protection. We live in a culture that doesn't care much for authority. We tend to want to do our own thing. We don't want anyone telling us what to do. The problem with that attitude is that it robs us of the benefits of rightly relating to authority. If you want the blessings of instruction, correction, direction, and protection, make a quality decision to work on your relationships with those in authority.

Are you receiving the four big benefits of being rightly related to those in authority over you?

*Let every soul be subject unto the higher powers. For there is no power but of God: the powers that be are ordained of God.* (Romans 13:1 KJV)

**Share the Glory**

Ronald Reagan was famous for having a certain sign on his desk, both as governor of California and as President. It read, "There's no limit to what we can accomplish if no one cares who gets the credit." One of the most neglected keys to growing an organization—and truly increasing in any type of relationship—is being willing to share the glory with other people. This truth is firmly rooted in the Bible. In Proverbs, we read: "Let another praise you and not your own mouth" (Proverbs 27:2). If you want to see maximum effort and loyalty from those around you, share the credit and do it publicly.

Are you willing to share the glory with others?

*For the body is not one member, but many.* (1 Corinthians 12:14 KJV)

# Hard Work Comes First

It's easy to envy people in the limelight and wish that we could have the same success as them. However, much of what we see broadcasted on television and social media is preceded by a lot of hard work. Brian Houston put it this way: "The 'chance of a lifetime' is usually built by many ordinary days of faithfulness. Our attitude in normal days is the path to extraordinary days." Today, I want to remind you that your "overnight success" will come through years of faithfulness. Don't pursue glory or the limelight, but pursue your dreams. Keep taking steps toward your goals, and one day, you'll find the breakthrough for which you've been waiting.

Can you see the value of hard work in your daily life?

*How joyful are those who fear the Lord—all who follow his ways! You will enjoy the fruit of your labor. How joyful and prosperous you will be!* (Psalm 128:1–2 NLT)

#  Jesus Believed in Others

The most influential person to walk the planet was Jesus of Nazareth—and what a leader He was. He handpicked a ragtag bunch of unpromising "average joes" and molded them into a force that has been shaking the world for two millennia. How did He do it? For one thing, He consistently showed that He believed in them. People tend to rise to the occasion when they know someone truly believes in them.

How can you show the people around you that you believe in them?

*Love never gives up, never loses faith, is always hopeful, and endures through every circumstance.* (1 Corinthians 13:7 NLT)

 **Judge Well**

Often, an ounce of judgment is worth a pound of genius. Look back across history at the greatest and best of the world's leaders and you'll notice something. They possessed good judgment—a quality the Bible often calls wisdom or discernment. In the book of Proverbs, Solomon writes, "My son, preserve sound judgment and discernment, do not let them out of your sight; they will be life for you, an ornament to grace your neck" (Proverbs 3:21–22). Good judgment is an important element in our lives. Winston Churchill once said, "Good and bad luck is a synonym in the great majority of instances for good and bad judgment."

## Have you let the Bible's wisdom improve your judgment?

*And this I pray, that your love may abound yet more and more in knowledge and in all judgment; That ye may approve things that are excellent; that ye may be sincere and without offence till the day of Christ....* (Philippians 1:9–10 KJV)

# 25 Answer Softly

Do you know people whose primary method of communication seems to be a verbal attack? The first words out of their mouths are usually an accusation or a question that puts you on the defensive. People who tend to communicate in the way I've just described are not necessarily bad people. They've simply developed that pattern of communication as a result of frustration, insecurity, or a feeling that they themselves are under attack. How should you respond to a verbal assault from such a person? The Bible says, "A soft answer turneth away wrath." The next time you're on the receiving end of an attack, instead of launching a counterattack, try a soft answer instead. The ability to defuse hostile communication will serve you well in life.

Are you willing to put an end to a verbal attack by providing a soft answer?

*A soft answer turneth away wrath: but grievous words stir up anger.*

(Proverbs 15:1 KJV)

## 26   Forgive

Too many of us have a mental list of what other people have done to us, and we drudge it up whenever they make a mistake. If you want to win in your relationships—whether it's in your marriage or in your friendships—remember what the writer of the book of Proverbs said, "He who covers a transgression seeks love, but he who repeats a matter separates friends." If your husband forgets to bring home flowers on your anniversary, don't hold it over him for the next 20 years. If your mother-in-law continually forgets that you hate potato salad, politely decline it at the dinner table and forgive her mistake. Never let another person's missteps keep you from allowing forgiveness in your life.

## Is forgiveness a ready part of your relationships?

*And when ye stand praying, forgive, if ye have ought against any: that your Father also which is in heaven may forgive you your trespasses.* (Mark 11:25 KJV)

# A Peaceful Environment

Have you ever felt like you worked in the middle of a "dog-eat-dog" atmosphere? It was just this type of atmosphere referred to in Galatians 5:15. It says, "If you keep on biting and devouring each other, watch out or you will be destroyed by each other." The good news is that you can break the cycle of backstabbing and competition in your workplace by making a decision to prefer others and treat them as you would want to be treated. God will honor that decision by bringing you increase and promotion. Your workplace will become more pleasant in the process.

Are you promoting peace within your organization?

*Blessed are the peacemakers: for they shall be called the children of God.*
(Matthew 5:9 KJV)

# Who Are You Recognizing?

Years ago, the National Retailers Association asked thousands of retail workers to list in order of importance their reasons for working where they did. Surprisingly, the number-one answer was "appreciation." Running a close second was "respect." Money came in a distant third. These results would have come as no surprise to Jesus. He clearly recognized the power of recognition.

> When was the last time you publicly praised a person you're trying to influence?

*And so he that had received five talents came and brought other five talents, saying, Lord, thou deliveredst unto me five talents: behold, I have gained beside them five talents more. His lord said unto him, Well done, thou good and faithful servant: thou hast been faithful over a few things, I will make thee ruler over many things: enter thou into the joy of thy lord.* (Matthew 25:20–21 KJV)

MARCH

Image • Baltimore Medina

# 1 Are You Progressing?

The first two months of a new year are behind us. Now would be a good time for you to stop and ask yourself some hard questions, such as: "What have I accomplished so far this year? Am I growing as a person? Am I making progress toward the goals I set for myself two months ago?" It's so easy to live day-to-day in survival mode and let the weeks slip away without doing any of the things that really matter. The apostle Paul set a wise example for us in that he established intermediate goals—he called them "marks" in Philippians 3:14—that helped him evaluate his progress.

## Are you progressing toward the goals you set for this year?

*Brethren, I count not myself to have apprehended: but this one thing I do, forgetting those things which are behind, and reaching forth unto those things which are before.* (Philippians 3:13 KJV)

# 2   Accountability

A common thread runs through Jesus' parables, especially those concerning delegated authority and money. That thread is accountability. In the stories Jesus told, people are held accountable for the diligence they applied and the results they produced. Great leaders follow this pattern. They hold people accountable for that which has been entrusted to them. Accountability is not about assigning blame. It's about helping people grow.

> Do those under your authority feel accountable or have they learned that a day of reckoning never comes?

*Live creatively, friends. If someone falls into sin, forgivingly restore him, saving your critical comments for yourself. You might be needing forgiveness before the day's out. Stoop down and reach out to those who are oppressed. Share their burdens, and so complete Christ's law. If you think you are too good for that, you are badly deceived.* (Galatians 6:1–3 Msg.)

# 3 Better Manage the Demands of Life

*Time* magazine once did a feature on stress and overcommitment. In the article, Dr. Joe Elkes stated, "Our mode of life itself, the way we live, is emerging as today's principle cause of illness." He's right. Too many people are achieving less yet feeling more stress. One of the key causes of this phenomenon is a failure to establish and maintain priorities. In the Bible, Jesus made many statements about the importance of priorities including, "Seek first the kingdom of God and all these things shall be added to you" (Matthew 6:33). Identifying right priorities and maintaining them is one of God's keys to managing stress and properly handling the demands of life.

Have you identified your top priorities and invested your time accordingly?

*Jesus said unto him, Thou shalt love the Lord thy God with all thy heart, and with all thy soul, and with all thy mind. This is the first and great commandment. And the second is like unto it, Thou shalt love thy neighbour as thyself. On these two commandments hang all the law and the prophets.* (Matthew 22:37–40 KJV)

# 4  Examine Your Choices

Your life is a reflection of the choices that you've made. If you want something to change, you first have to take responsibility for what is going on in your life. As Steven Covey wrote in *The 7 Habits of Highly Effective People*, "Until a person can say deeply and honestly, 'I am what I am today because of the choices I made yesterday,' that person cannot say, 'I choose otherwise.'" The Bible talks about our power of choice in Deuteronomy 30:19: "I call heaven and earth to record this day against you, that I have set before you life and death, blessing and cursing: therefore choose life...." It can't be much clearer than that. If you want good things in your life, make good, life-filled decisions.

Have you taken responsibility for your life or are you blaming circumstances or people around you?

*The heart of man plans his way, but the Lord establishes his steps.*
(Proverbs 16:9 ESV)

# 5   The Power of Consultation

Robert Louis Stevenson once wrote, "Marriage is like life in this—that it is a field of battle, and not a bed of roses." I'm saddened to say that statement is true for too many marriages, but it doesn't have to be true of yours. One of the characteristics common to winning marriages is the habit of consultation. It means that you and your spouse consult each other on decisions and refuse to act until you're in agreement. Men and women approach problems differently. When you get in the habit of consulting with each other until you're in agreement, you'll make better decisions and enjoy more peace. Your marriage will be more like a bed of roses than a field of battle.

Are you making decisions alone or consulting your spouse?

*For by wise guidance you can wage your war, and in abundance of counselors there is victory.* (Proverbs 24:6 ESV)

# 6 The Light of God

Some people assume God can only be found in visible miracles and answered prayers. If they can't detect Him in the areas they'd like, they assume He doesn't exist or doesn't care. However, they're working from an incorrect assumption. God is omnipresent, everywhere at all times. Consider how sunlight is immediately available to the parts of earth facing the sun. It's in all places immediately, unless people turn away or take shelter. That light is similar to God's presence. He is everywhere at once, quietly bringing growth to those who are planted and warmth to those open to Him. You can't always see Him at work, but you can see the effects.

Where have you seen God at work in big and small ways in your life and in the lives of those around you?

*This is the message we heard from Jesus and now declare to you: God is light, and there is no darkness in him at all.* (1 John 1:5 NLT)

# God Makes You Able

Many people don't realize that they themselves are the biggest obstacle standing between them and their dreams. Henry Ford once said, "Whether you think you can or you think you can't, you're right." The Bible concurs with this statement. Proverbs 23:7 says, "For as [a man] thinketh in his heart, so is he." God has placed dreams of greatness inside every one of us, and He's equipped us to pursue those dreams, one step at a time. Maybe you want to be a school teacher or a CEO or the best stay-at-home mom you can be. Whatever it is, purpose to consistently pursue your passion. Picture yourself becoming exactly the person you want to be, and you'll propel yourself to realize the dream inside of you. Perseverance is key to victory in your life.

## What doubts have kept you from pursuing your dreams?

*I have strength for all things in Christ Who empowers me [I am ready for anything and equal to anything through Him Who infuses inner strength into me; I am self-sufficient in Christ's sufficiency].* (Philippians 4:13 Amp.)

# 8 Everyone Can Win

There is a book in the business world titled *The Ruthless Leader*. That title pretty much sums up the cutthroat, win-at-any-price mentality that a lot of us think of when we talk about winning. According to that way of thinking, when someone wins, it means everyone else has to lose. We're told we'll have to climb over people to get to the top and put others down in order to put ourselves over. That's not winning as God defines it. In God's system, you don't win over people; you win over circumstances. When you win God's way, it's never lonely at the top.

> Do you feel someone else has to lose in order for you to win?

For everyone who has been born of God overcomes the world. And this is the victory that has overcome the world—our faith. (1 John 5:4 ESV)

## 9   Pray for Wisdom

How would you like to be known around the office as a person who always makes sound decisions? How would it affect your performance and satisfaction on the job if you had access to great wisdom whenever you had a decision to make? The truth is, we all have access to such wisdom. It's just that most of us don't know it or utilize it. In the book of James, we're told, "If any of you lacks wisdom, he should ask God, who gives generously to all without finding fault, and it will be given to him." An important key to being happy in your job is knowing you can call on God for wisdom. Pray for wisdom on the job. You'll enjoy your work more and enjoy more success.

Have you asked God to help you on the job?

*If any of you lack wisdom, let him ask of God, that giveth to all men liberally, and upbraideth not; and it shall be given him.* (James 1:5 KJV)

What Not to Do in Your Communication

No one likes to be manipulated. Manipulation causes people to shut down the flow of communication. One good way to test your conversation for traces of manipulation is to listen for the words "should," "ought," and "must." When you catch yourself trying to influence others by telling them they "ought" to do something, you're using guilt as a tool and have stepped over into manipulation. Winning communicators choose, instead, to keep the lines of influence open.

*Do not take advantage of each other, but fear your God. I am the Lord your God.* (Leviticus 25:17 NIV)

Are you willing to eliminate manipulative speech from your communication?

Image • Donny Jiang

#  Become Like Jesus

People of great influence tend to be trustworthy, unconditional in their acceptance of others, effective communicators, and skillful at conflict resolution. These traits give you the ability to guide your children, move ahead on the job, and have a positive impact on all with whom you come in contact. No other person on earth has ever exhibited these qualities to greater degree than Jesus of Nazareth. If you want to be a person of influence, you'll find no better pattern than Him.

## Are you influencing people like Jesus did?

*Let each of you esteem and look upon and be concerned for not [merely] his own interests, but also each for the interests of others. Let this same attitude and purpose and [humble] mind be in you which was in Christ Jesus: [let Him be your example in humility].* (Philippians 2:4–5 Amp.)

# 12 Live for Something Beyond Yourself

William Booth had a passion to help the homeless; that passion led him to start the Salvation Army. Clara Barton's compassion gave her the idea for the American Red Cross. Booth and Barton were filled with great purpose, but they weren't born that way. They deliberately developed themselves to become the people they were. You can do the same thing. Take your eyes off your everyday struggles and look for God's high purpose for you. Involve yourself in causes that propel you toward your true destiny. You'll win great victories, reap great rewards, and inspire others as you relentlessly follow your God-given passion.

## What purpose in life are you striving toward?

*Learn to do right! Seek justice, relieve the oppressed, and correct the oppressor. Defend the fatherless, plead for the widow.* (Isaiah 1:17 Amp.)

# The Importance of One Soul

Although preachers will be rewarded for the work they do reaching many people at once, your work influencing people around you is just as important. That's why Jesus told a story about the shepherd who left 99 sheep to go search for one missing sheep. Luke 15:7 says, "There is more joy in heaven over one lost sinner who repents and returns to God than over ninety-nine others who are righteous and haven't strayed away!" Start a party in heaven: reach one person for God.

> What do you value most: being seen by people or bringing one person to Jesus?

*What man of you, having an hundred sheep, if he lose one of them, doth not leave the ninety and nine in the wilderness, and go after that which is lost, until he find it? And when he hath found it, he layeth it on his shoulders, rejoicing. And when he cometh home, he calleth together his friends and neighbours, saying unto them, Rejoice with me; for I have found my sheep which was lost.*
(Luke 15:4–6 KJV)

# 14 The Gospel Is Good

What do you think of when you hear the word "gospel"? Do you think of a certain style of music? Do you associate the word with tent preachers and revival meetings? The actual meaning of the word may surprise you. The word "gospel" is a word from the Bible that simply means "good news." What is this good news? It is that God is for you; He loves you and has provided a way to make your life better. That's why Paul was able to say, "I am not ashamed of the gospel for it is the power of God for salvation, deliverance, and rescue to everyone who believes." Wherever you are at this point in your life, God wants to make it better. He wants you to be well. He wants you to prosper. That, my friend, is good news.

Are you ready to share the good news of the Gospel with someone today?

*For I am not ashamed of the gospel of Christ: for it is the power of God unto salvation to every one that believeth; to the Jew first, and also to the Greek.*
(Romans 1:16 KJV)

## 15 Raising Your Children

Parents, if you haven't yet noticed, our society is prepared to raise your kids instead of you. Television, movies, friends—even our schools—will influence your children in a way that might not line up with your family's values. Don't allow that to happen. You certainly can't isolate your children from society, but you can pro-actively be a part of their lives so when society presents them with a contradictory agenda, your children will be able to discern what is right and what is wrong. You can teach your children values and encourage them to bring questions to you. Proverbs 22:6 says, "Train a child in the way he should go, and when he is old he will not turn from it." If you want to win in your family, choose to raise your children proactively from your home.

## Who is raising your kids?

*Discipline your son, and he will give you rest; he will give delight to your heart.* (Proverbs 29:17 ESV)

## See Things Differently

What made Jesus the greatest impacter of people the world has ever known? One trait Jesus exhibited was the courage to see things differently. On two occasions in which He raised someone from the dead, Jesus resisted using the term "dead." He told one grieving father, "Your daughter is not dead. She's sleeping." His unique perspective revolutionized situations. Let's learn from His example.

### What problem can you start seeing differently today?

*But when he had sent them all out, he took the child's father and mother, along with his companions, and entered the child's room. He clasped the girl's hand and said, "Talitha koum," which means, "Little girl, get up." At that, she was up and walking around!* (Mark 5:37–42 Msg.)

# 17 Keys to Integrity

Maintaining absolute integrity is the bottom-line rule for leaders if they want those under them to follow them under all conditions. How do you cultivate integrity? First: Keep your word. If you say something, make certain it is the exact truth. Second: Choose the harder right over the easier wrong. When you are faced with choices of right or wrong, no matter what your boss thinks, no matter what the stockholders think, choose the right. The Bible is clear on this issue: To lead effectively, especially during difficult times, you must be known as a person of your word.

## What is your reputation for integrity?

*Better is the poor that walketh in his integrity, than he that is perverse in his lips, and is a fool.* (Proverbs 19:1 KJV)

# 18 Discipline

A generation ago, old-fashioned discipline became unfashionable. "Let kids do their own thing," we were told. Today, we're paying a high price for that philosophy. The cost is exacted in the form of broken homes, high-crime rates, and swelling prison populations. The Bible says that to withhold discipline from your child is to hate him, but that diligent, appropriate discipline is an expression of love. Children need direction and correction because they're immature—physically, emotionally, and spiritually. It will enhance their prospects for success and help make your house a home.

## Will you dare to discipline your kids in love?

*He that spareth his rod hateth his son: but he that loveth him chasteneth him betimes.* (Proverbs 13:24 KJV)

# 19 Agape Love

The Greeks had four different words to express the concept of love. One of those four is your key to building stronger relationships. One of the words the Greeks had for love is "eros." It refers to romantic, physical love, and it's what most people in our culture think about when they hear the word "love." The word "storge" describes the love a parent naturally has for a child. "Phileo" refers to the affectionate feeling of love. But the Greeks had a fourth word for love, and it's the word used in the New Testament every time it mentions God's love for us. That word is "agape." It would be accurate to say that "agape" is the God kind of love. It's defined as the kind of love that gives, even to the point of laying down one's life for another. It's an action, not a feeling. It's the kind of love that will transform all your relationships to sources of blessing and joy.

## What kind of love fuels your relationships?

*For God so loved the world, that he gave his only begotten Son, that whosoever believeth in him should not perish, but have everlasting life.* (John 3:16 KJV)

#  Untimely Speech

Babies have the amazing ability to stick both feet in their mouths. We adults often exhibit the same talent. People largely gauge your leadership by what you say. If you continually make comments which offend or cause confusion, others may question your ability to lead. The Bible says the most mature leaders are those who are able to control their tongues. It tells us that wise speech is peace loving, considerate, and sincere. Apply these standards, and your speech will show maturity and others will respond to your leadership.

How often do you put your foot in your mouth?

*The tongue of the wise useth knowledge aright: but the mouth of fools poureth out foolishness.* (Proverbs 15:2 KJV)

## 21 Godly Plans

Did you know that God is a planner? Many people think they don't need clearly defined plans in order to be successful. They want to fly through life by the seat of their pants. But I'm here to tell you that God uses planning and so should you. All through the Bible, we see God laying out a specific plan and then working to bring it to pass. In the account of creation, God says, "Let us make man in our image." He established the goal of creating a being that would be crafted in the very likeness of God Himself. Then He set about achieving that goal. It's a pattern we see repeated over and over in the Bible. Follow God's example: set clear goals, write them down, and then go to work.

Have you established
godly plans in your life?

*Good planning and hard work lead to prosperity, but hasty shortcuts lead to poverty.* (Proverbs 21:5 NLT)

 Be Teachable

I once heard someone described as having "a mind like a steel trap...always tightly closed." I've found the older we get, the more likely we are to become closed to new ideas and new ways of looking at things. That's unfortunate because remaining teachable is one of the most important things you can do to facilitate success in this life. Proverbs 12:15 says it this way: "The way of a fool seems right to him, but a wise man listens to advice." According to God, thinking you already know everything is foolish. God wants learning and growing to be something we do, not just when we're young, but for a lifetime.

Are you teachable?

*Whoso loveth instruction loveth knowledge: but he that hateth reproof is brutish.*
(Proverbs 12:1 KJV)

# 23 A Love That Gives

A popular song in the 80s asked, "What's love got to do with it?" A lot of people ask the same question when it comes to growing as a relational leader. They ask it because they don't understand the Bible definition of love. Of all the concepts in the English language, none is as overused and under comprehended as "love." When the Bible encourages us to love others, it's not talking about a syrupy, emotion. It's talking about the willingness to give sacrificially. That's why love is a key element in growing as a relational leader.

## What are you doing most in your relationships: giving or taking?

*Unfailing love and faithfulness protect the king; his throne is made secure through love.* (Proverbs 20:28 NLT)

#  The Pitfall of Pride

After years of a downturn in revenue, a restaurant owner in Ohio found herself close to half a million dollars in debt. Her restaurant was failing partially because the food wasn't that good and partially because she knew nothing about running a restaurant. The irony was that her own brother was a chef with thirty years of experience who would have helped his sister if she had only asked. Years later, when someone asked her why she never approached her brother about the situation, she admitted it was because of pride. If she had only realized how much stress she would have to deal with as her restaurant crumbled, perhaps she would have chosen humility in the first place.

## Have you allowed pride to keep you from advancing in life?

*But he giveth more grace. Wherefore he saith, God resisteth the proud, but giveth grace unto the humble.* (James 4:6 KJV)

## 25 Define Reality Correctly

According to some business writers, "defining reality" is the primary job of every CEO. The best leaders tend to be those who are best at assessing the situation objectively. Leaders who fail to define reality accurately rarely lead effectively. Many of the greatest leaders in the Bible had this quality. For example, the greatest leader of all time, Jesus of Nazareth, consistently defined reality for His disciples. Like Jesus, effective leaders are sensitive to others' feelings, but they don't hold up a wet finger to the winds of opinion. They lead.

How would you rate your ability to assess the situation and communicate it to others?

*These things I have spoken unto you, that in me ye might have peace. In the world ye shall have tribulation: but be of good cheer; I have overcome the world.* (John 16:33 KJV)

# We Need Each Other

The people around you are valuable. They are not pawns to push around on your way to the top or people to walk over whenever you want. They have gifts and talents that can enhance your life. If you want to win in your relationships, know that God gave you your family and friends for a reason. As John Donne wrote, "No man is an island, entire of itself; every man is a piece of the continent, a part of the main."

Have you recognized how the people around you play a supporting role in your life?

*On the contrary, those parts of the body that seem to be weaker are indispensable, and the parts that we think are less honorable we treat with special honor... so that there should be no division in the body, but that its parts should have equal concern for each other.* (1 Corinthians 12:22–23, 25 KJV)

#  Maintain Perspective

When you lose perspective, you lose momentum and give yourself the opportunity to quit. Thomas Edison once stated, "I haven't failed. I've just found 10,000 ways that won't work." His choice to maintain a positive perspective is the reason he was able to create over 1,000 patents. Too many people stop when they don't see success, even though the next time they tried, they might have won. Harriet Beecher Stowe put it this way: "When you get into a tight place and everything goes against you... till it seems as though you could not hang on a minute longer, never give up then, for that is just the place and time that the tide will turn."

How do you view impossibilities that come your way: as difficulties you'll never get through or opportunities for God to impact your life?

*Be strong, and let your heart take courage, all you who wait for the Lord!*
(Psalm 31:24 ESV)

#  Can You See Opportunity?

Winston Churchill once said, "An optimist sees an opportunity in every calamity. A pessimist sees a calamity in every opportunity." Which approach do you tend to take? Great leaders tend to see opportunities—even in difficult times. They have trained themselves to look at every situation and see what's possible. For example, the Bible's King David showed an amazing ability to devise creative solutions for military and administrative problems. It was an ability he knew that came from seeking God's wisdom.

> Have you sought God's wisdom for seeing opportunity in calamity?

*If any of you lack wisdom, let him ask of God, that giveth to all men liberally, and upbraideth not; and it shall be given him.* (James 1:5 KJV)

**Be Friendly First**

In his bestselling book, *How to Win Friends and Influence People*, Dale Carnegie wrote, "You can make more friends in two months by becoming interested in other people than you can in two years by trying to get other people interested in you." The Bible is filled with verses that agree with this truth. For example, Paul writes in Philippians chapter 2, "Let each of you look not only to his own interests, but also to the interests of others," and in 1 Corinthians chapter 10, "Don't be concerned for your own good but for the good of others." Both the Word and the world agree: putting others before your own self is key to winning in your relationships.

Which saying better describes your heart in the relationships God has brought into your life— "What's in this for me?" or "What can I do for you?"

*Bear ye one another's burdens, and so fulfil the law of Christ.* (Galatians 6:2 KJV)

# Increase Your Responsiveness

Leaders can't expect those they lead to be responsive to their authority if they reflect a rebellious attitude toward their own leaders. That's why the Bible tells us to honor and respect all authority.

> If you want to reap greater responsiveness to your leadership, why not try sowing more responsiveness to those you serve?

*Submit yourselves to every ordinance of man for the Lord's sake: whether it be to the king, as supreme; or unto governors, as unto them that are sent by him for the punishment of evildoers, and for the praise of them that do well. For so is the will of God, that with well doing ye may put to silence the ignorance of foolish men:* (1 Peter 2:13–15 KJV)

# 31 Put Down Your Phone

With all the electronic forms of communication we have nowadays, it's easy to get caught up in our to-do lists and texts and forget that a hurting world is out there who needs us to show them the love of Jesus. The waiter at your local restaurant won't see you as an example of the love of Jesus unless you turn off your cell phone and take time to interact with him. Your neighbors will appreciate an invite to church much more if you've taken time to get to know them personally. The cashier having a bad day could stay depressed unless you end your phone call and ask how she's doing instead. Technology is wonderful, but keep in mind that electronics can never replace kindness and interpersonal communication.

Do your actions show people are more important to you than technology?

*A new commandment I give to you, that you love one another: just as I have loved you, you also are to love one another. By this all people will know that you are my disciples, if you have love for one another.* (John 13:34–35 ESV)

APRIL

Image • Porter Ellenburg

# 1  Engage With Your Children

How well do you know your children? That may sound like an odd question, but it has been my experience that far too many people struggle in their roles as parents simply because they haven't invested the time and attention necessary to discover who their children are as God created them. In Proverbs chapter 20, wise parents are encouraged to "observe" their children. Successful parents have open ears and eyes. They study each child and discover their interests, abilities, patterns, and pitfalls. Don't assume you know them just because they live under your roof; take time to find out who God has created them to be.

> Have you taken the time to discover who it is you're trying to raise?

*How precious also are thy thoughts unto me, O God! how great is the sum of them! If I should count them, they are more in number than the sand: when I awake, I am still with thee.* (Psalm 139:17–18 KJV)

# 2 God Created You to Win

Would you agree that God is a winner? Most people who have the sense to recognize the existence of God would agree that He's a winner in every sense of the Word. Yet we, very often, don't see ourselves as winners, even though we're told in Genesis that God made us in His image and likeness. The first marching orders God gave mankind were, "Subdue the earth and have dominion over it." In other words, He said, "Go out there and win!" Whatever challenges you may be facing today, you can be confident that God created you to overcome them.

## Are you seeing yourself as God sees you?

*And God blessed them, and God said unto them, Be fruitful, and multiply, and replenish the earth, and subdue it: and have dominion over the fish of the sea, and over the fowl of the air, and over every living thing that moveth upon the earth.* (Genesis 1:28 KJV)

# 3 Build Upon Your Past

During World War II, Corrie ten Boom provided refuge for Jewish fugitives. After being found out by the Nazis, she was imprisoned for ten months in a concentration camp. Thanks to a "clerical error of man and a miracle of God," she was released from that camp in 1944. She certainly could have lived the rest of her life out of bitterness and hate from all she had experienced, but instead, she used her past as a building block for the future. She reached out to those affected in harsh ways by the trauma of the war. She used what should have killed her to save the lives of others, both physically and spiritually. I want to encourage you today to never let your past take you down; instead, let it build you into a better person.

How do you view your past: something that will take you down or something that will prepare you for the future?

*And we know that all things work together for good to them that love God, to them who are the called according to his purpose.* (Romans 8:28 KJV)

#  Comfort

At one time or another, all of us need to be comforted. We live in a fallen world in which evil is still very much on the loose. That's why it's vital that you understand the source of all true comfort. That source is God. In fact, 2 Corinthians chapter 1 describes Him as "the God of all comfort." The next time you experience loss, disappointment, emotional hurt, or pain, turn to the one who is best equipped to bring comfort to bear in your situation—turn to God.

> When hurting, will you let God comfort you with the comfort only He can bring?

*Blessed be God, even the Father of our Lord Jesus Christ, the Father of mercies, and the God of all comfort; Who comforteth us in all our tribulation, that we may be able to comfort them which are in any trouble, by the comfort wherewith we ourselves are comforted of God.* (2 Corinthians 1:3–4 KJV)

# 5   Happy on the Job

Your level of happiness in your work has a huge impact on your quality of life. As a pastor, I frequently counsel frustrated people who are blaming other people in their lives, when the truth is, unhappiness on the job is eating them up inside. One of the most liberating things you can know is that God wants you to be happy in your work. Isaiah 65:22 says, "My people shall long enjoy the work of their hands." Why is your work important? Because it goes a long way toward defining who you are. We all derive a great deal of our identities from our jobs.

## Is frustration on the job standing between you and true fulfillment?

*May the favor of the Lord our God rest on us; establish the work of our hands for us—yes, establish the work of our hands.* (Psalm 90:17 NIV)

#  Negotiation and Parenting

If you have ever found yourself negotiating with a three-year-old and losing, you know how important it is to have influence in the lives of your children. Believe it or not, negotiation, or "conflict resolution," is a natural part of raising children. In this regard, the Bible says, "...provoke not your children to anger, lest they be discouraged." The iron fist may seem effective in the short run, but it will ultimately prove counterproductive. There's a way to be firm with your children without pushing them into discouragement.

## Have you learned the biblical key to conflict resolution with your kids?

*And, ye fathers, provoke not your children to wrath: but bring them up in the nurture and admonition of the Lord.* (Ephesians 6:4 KJV)

## 7 Focus on Others

Many people are unintentionally alienated from others because they don't know how to hold a conversation. When talking with other people, they talk about themselves, their hobbies, their kids, and their opinions—to the extent that they completely ignore other people. They may be looking at them and expecting a response, but they have forgotten the golden rule of conversation: actively engage with and be genuinely interested in the people to whom you are talking. That means you need to stop talking about yourself and think of questions that will allow others to talk about their hobbies, likes, dislikes, and so on. Whether you're talking to close friends or acquaintances, directing conversations toward others will help you win in relationships every time.

Who are your conversations focused around—you or the people around you?

*Through patience a ruler can be persuaded, and a gentle tongue can break a bone.* (Proverbs 25:15 NIV)

# 8 Don't Accuse

At some point in our lives, we've all experienced the truth that accusations can be harmful. People blame others of doing something wrong, whether or not it's reality. The danger in this is that accusations plant ideas in people's minds that may or may not be true. Opinions are formed based off those accusations. Englishman Thomas Fuller once said, "Even doubtful accusations leave a stain behind them." When you accuse someone, in essence, you are believing the worst about that person. A winning relationship requires that we believe the best about other people. If you want to win in your relationships, I encourage you to find out the truth about a situation and keep accusations far from your communication.

## What can you do to ensure that accusations stay out of your mouth?

*You shall not bear false witness against your neighbor.* (Exodus 20:16 ESV)

# 9 Leaders Build the Future

When it comes to finding potential leaders in your organization, it is vital to look for those who know how to catch vision. When you talk to people about the future, you want their eyes to light up. A person who doesn't feel the thrill of a challenge is not a potential leader. On more than one occasion, Jesus said, "Let him who has ears to hear, let him hear."

> Are you promoting leaders who hear and respond to your vision?

*Then I said to them, You see the bad situation we are in—how Jerusalem lies in ruins, and its gates are burned with fire. Come, let us build up the wall of Jerusalem, that we may no longer be a disgrace. Then I told them of the hand of my God which was upon me for good, and also the words that the king had spoken to me. And they said, Let us rise up and build! So they strengthened their hands for the good work.* (Nehemiah 2:17–18 Amp.)

**Stand by Your Beliefs**

In the fourth century AD, the Church was in a heated debate. People were questioning the divinity of Jesus. A man named Athanasius knew this core truth of Christianity could not be redefined. He spent his life fighting against this heresy called Arianism, despite being exiled and forced to flee for his life many times. Author Lawrence Kimbrough pointed out, "The Church today would be a different kind of place if not for a short, dark-skinned, red-bearded half-hermit who singlehandedly fought an empire for the truth of the gospel." Athanasius lived with unparalleled conviction for the truth of his beliefs.

## Are you willing to stand by your beliefs?

*Blessed are ye, when men shall revile you, and persecute you, and shall say all manner of evil against you falsely, for my sake. Rejoice, and be exceeding glad: for great is your reward in heaven: for so persecuted they the prophets which were before you.* (Matthew 5:11–12 KJV)

## 11  Seek Councel

In Proverbs 15:22 King Solomon writes, "Plans fail for lack of counsel, but with many advisers they succeed." What are your plans? Are you thinking of starting a new business venture? Undertaking an ambitious project? According to God's wisdom book, you can greatly increase your prospects for success by seeking out wise counsel. That doesn't mean going out and randomly surveying your friends and relatives. It means seeking out those who know where you're headed and know how to help you get there.

Have you searched for good counsel in your life?

*Where no counsel is, the people fall: but in the multitude of counsellors there is safety.* (Proverbs 11:14 KJV)

# Check Your Timing

How many times have you heard this phrase: "Timing is everything"? Clearly, when it comes to organizational planning, timing should always be a consideration. Wise King Solomon tells us in Ecclesiastes that there is an appropriate time for everything in life. Timing was key in the success of Jesus, and you can make it work for you too. Major announcements should be timed for maximum impact. New products should be introduced at the most opportune time. Timing should also be a consideration in releasing the occasional bad news every organization has from time to time.

## How's your timing?

*To everything there is a season, and a time for every matter or purpose under heaven.* (Ecclesiastes 3:1 Amp.)

## 13   When Needed, Ask for Help

Some people would rather do a job wrong than swallow their pride and ask for help. How would you like to be treated by a doctor who refused to ask for help when he wasn't sure what course of action to take? You wouldn't let such a doctor prescribe medicine for you, much less operate on you. Yet many people in other types of jobs won't ask for more information when they need it. An important key to being happy on the job is knowing when to ask for help or more information. Proverbs 24:5 says, "A man of knowledge increases power, and in the abundance of counselors there is victory." Want to find happiness and success on the job? Ask for help when you need it.

> Are you humble enough to ask for help when you need it?

*And I said to [him], If it pleases the king and if your servant has found favor in your sight, I ask that you will send me to Judah, to the city of my fathers' sepulchers, that I may rebuild it.* (Nehemiah 2:5 Amp.)

# Above Average

Aristotle defined happiness as "full use of the powers God gave you along the lines of excellence." In saying that, he was echoing what the Bible had stated 700 years earlier. Proverbs says, "Poor is he who works with a negligent hand, but the hand of the diligent makes rich." A common trait of those who experience lasting success in this life is a passion for excellence. "Just good enough to get by" is not enough for them. Average is not acceptable. Excellence is the only option.

Which word better describes your efforts in life: excellence or mediocrity?

*Whatever you do in word or deed, do all in the name of the Lord Jesus, giving thanks through Him to God the Father.* (Colossians 3:17 NASB)

## 15 Constructive Discontent

One of the traits you should look for in a potential leader in your organization is a constructive spirit of discontent. Being constructively discontent is very different from being critical. When people say, "There has to be a better way to do this," you can see if there's leadership potential by asking, "Have you ever thought about what that better way might be?" When people say "no," they're being critical, not constructive. People who are comfortable in the status quo are not leaders. People who look for ways to go beyond what is normal have leadership potential.

> Do the people you're considering for a promotion believe there's always a better way to do things?

*But select from all the people some capable, honest men who fear God and hate bribes. Appoint them as leaders over groups of one thousand, one hundred, fifty, and ten. (Exodus 18:21 NLT)*

#  Self-Restraint and Authority Matter

Many people don't want to admit there's reason for self-restraint. They prefer the "freedom" offered through a life of no rules. Problems arise when people decide they can ignore rules—and authority is snubbed as tyrannical. However, respecting authority is the best path to peace. Listen to how the apostle Paul worded it. "Do you want to be on good terms with the government? Be a responsible citizen and you'll get on just fine, the government working to your advantage. ...Live responsibly—not just to avoid punishment but also because it's the right way to live." Our job is to live wisely; the government is there to protect our right to do so.

## What is one way you can choose to live responsibly today?

*But if you're breaking the rules right and left, watch out. The police aren't there just to be admired in their uniforms. God also has an interest in keeping order, and he uses them to do it.* (Romans 13:4 Msg.)

## Take Responsibility

If you are interested in being promoted in the workplace, one of the most important traits to embody is a willingness to shoulder responsibility. So many spend their energies looking for ways to avoid additional responsibility; few actually seek it out. Carrying responsibility doesn't need to intimidate you. You can discover the joy of accomplishment. In fact, contributing to the success of the team is a reward in itself. Employers are always on the lookout for people who understand this. They are the ones who will be moved to positions of leadership.

Are you willing to tackle
new challenges?

*But let every man prove his own work, and then shall he have rejoicing in himself alone, and not in another. For every man shall bear his own burden.*
(Galatians 6:4–5 KJV)

# Your Job Is a Gift

Some people spring out of bed in the morning. They can't wait to get to work. Others dread the morning alarm. Some people find fulfillment and reward in their work. Others are simply "working for the weekend." With which group of people do you most closely identify? If you want to find happiness on the job, you need to start with one important attitude adjustment. You must accept work as a gift from God, not a punishment. You'll never find contentment in any job as long as you consider that job a curse rather than a blessing. When you begin to look at your work as a God-given opportunity for promotion, your whole approach to work will begin to change for the better.

## What does your job mean to you?

*And it is a good thing to receive wealth from God and the good health to enjoy it. To enjoy your work and accept your lot in life—this is indeed a gift from God.* (Ecclesiastes 5:19 NLT)

# 19 Cover Your Spouse

Have you ever heard the saying, "Love covers a multitude of sins?" It's from the Bible, and it points us to a significant key in cultivating a winning marriage. Partners in a successful marriage "cover" one another. What does it mean to "cover" your spouse? It means you don't point out or expose his/her weaknesses, shortcomings, or mistakes. Whenever I hear a husband make his wife the butt of a joke or a wife criticize her husband in front of friends, I cringe. It tells me they haven't learned the value of covering one another. If you love your spouse, you will cover them.

## Can your spouse count on you to cover his or her shortcomings?

*And above all things have fervent charity among yourselves: for charity shall cover the multitude of sins.* (1 Peter 4:8 KJV)

# Are Your Ears Open?

Studies show that most of us are only 25 percent as good at listening as we are at talking. Shakespeare called it "the disease of not listening." The symptoms of the disease are strained relationships, faulty information, unwise decisions, and lots of wasted time and energy. It seems more of us need to take the James 1:19 cure in which the Bible encourages us to "be swift to listen and slow to speak." We'll find ourselves to be better informed, better motivators of people, and more likely to be listened to because we made others feel important.

## How are your listening skills?

*Even a fool, when he holdeth his peace, is counted wise: and he that shutteth his lips is esteemed a man of understanding.* (Proverbs 17:28 KJV)

## 21  Positive Thinking Goes Far

A 62-year-old woman became lost in the Sierra Nevada after a hike with friends. Despite falling and fracturing a bone, she survived nine days lost before being rescued, treated at a hospital, and released. Do you know what kept her going? A positive attitude. Your attitude will propel you further than you think you can go or take you down sooner than you want. As philosopher William James once said, "The greatest discovery of any generation is that a human being can alter his life by altering his attitude." People of character recognize the need for positivity.

Have you unleashed the power
of a positive attitude?

*A merry heart doeth good like a medicine: but a broken spirit drieth the bones.*
(Proverbs 17:22 KJV)

When You and Your Leader Disagree

Sometimes leaders make decisions that we don't like. We disagree with it principally or we think there's a better way. The biggest trap people fall into when they disagree with a decision is that they disrespect their leaders because they disagree. That's a dangerous attitude to have. The Bible tells us time and again that we need to respect and pray for those in authority over us. Unless they are telling us to do something unbiblical, we need to follow their lead and pray for them to be used by God. The decisions they make won't be perfect, but you can trust God to use your leaders as you respect the office in which they stand.

What is your first course of action if you disagree with those in authority over you?

*I exhort therefore, that, first of all, supplications, prayers, intercessions, and giving of thanks, be made for all men; for kings, and for all that are in authority; that we may lead a quiet and peaceable life in all godliness and honesty. For this is good and acceptable in the sight of God our Saviour....* (1 Timothy 2:1–3 KJV)

# 23  Prove Yourself Trustworthy

When people reveal their deepest thoughts and feelings to someone, their defenses are down and, at that moment, they are highly vulnerable. When others become vulnerable and disclose their hearts to you, how do you respond? It can be devastating if they feel ridiculed or rejected in any way. So, you must prove yourself trustworthy. Respond by accepting what they say and opening your own heart to them in return. It's precisely the way God deals with us.

Are you building trust by responding correctly in the moment of disclosure?

*Young men likewise exhort to be sober minded. In all things shewing thyself a pattern of good works: in doctrine shewing uncorruptness, gravity, sincerity, sound speech, that cannot be condemned; that he that is of the contrary part may be ashamed, having no evil thing to say of you.* (Titus 2:6–8 KJV)

#  Spend Your Time Wisely

If you visit Big Ben in London, you'll find a little poem about the preciousness of time inscribed at the base of the clock tower. It reads, "No minute lost ever comes back again. Take heed and see you do nothing in vain." Time is precious. That's why one of the most crucial lessons we can learn is how to use time wisely. John D. Rockefeller once said, "Without the management of time, you will soon have nothing left to manage." On a similar note, the Bible encourages us to "redeem the time," which simply means we should put it to the best use possible.

*So be careful how you live. Don't live like fools, but like those who are wise. Make the most of every opportunity in these evil days.* (Ephesians 5:15–16 NLT)

How much of each precious day are you spending wisely?

 Sacrifice

Sacrifice. It's the willingness to set aside personal comfort for the sake of others. It's one of the rarest commodities in the earth today. That's why it is all the more vital parents instill this quality in their children. Here's why: The law of sowing and reaping is immutable. As Jesus said, "Give and it shall be given unto you." In other words, the standard of measure we use in helping others will be the standard by which we are helped.

*Are you teaching your children how vital it is to give up some things in order to make a difference in the lives of others?*

*Do nothing from factional motives [through contentiousness, strife, selfishness, or for unworthy ends] or prompted by conceit and empty arrogance. Instead, in the true spirit of humility (lowliness of mind) let each regard the others as better than and superior to himself [thinking more highly of one another than you do of yourselves]. (Philippians 2:3 Amp.)*

#  26  When Life Gets Difficult

When one of my friends was training for his first marathon, he received specific race-day advice. "On mile 10, you will see people in much better shape than you falling along the side with muscle cramps. You'll think, 'If they're having that much trouble, I'll never make it.' But don't let them get into your head. Stay hydrated, and you'll be fine." Sure enough, when Tim reached mile 10, that's exactly what happened—but because he'd been warned, he kept going. You may not be preparing for a marathon, but you are in the middle of a race called life. When you see someone else falter, don't doubt what you are doing. Keep going, keep pursuing your dream, and always remember: If you don't quit, you will win.

When things get difficult and you see others who give up, do you allow that to steer you off course?

*Do not, therefore, fling away your fearless confidence, for it carries a great and glorious compensation of reward.* (Hebrews 10:35 Amp.)

# 27 Words Matter

It's not what you say that matters; it's what you do. Right? Wrong. Of all the assumptions you can make, one of the most dangerous is the assumption that words don't matter. According to the Bible, words are alive. The words you speak changes things. They frame your future. And they have a huge impact on those around you. Blaise Pascal wrote, "Cold words freeze people and hot words scorch them, and bitter words make them bitter, and wrathful words make them wrathful. ... Kind words also produce their own image on men's souls and a beautiful image it is. They soothe, and quiet, and comfort the hearer." The belief that words don't matter is another false assumption that will keep you from winning in life.

Do you fully understand the power available to you through your words?

*Wise words are more valuable than much gold and many rubies.*
(Proverbs 20:15 NLT)

Encourage Yourself

Believe it or not, you can give yourself open heart surgery, but you won't need a scalpel. All you need are words. Every star athlete and successful business person knows the value of giving one's self a good pep talk. It's the fastest way to rebuild your confidence. You can talk yourself right through a mountain of doubts and disappointments. In short, you can use your mouth to change your heart. That truth is straight from the Bible. It says that belief comes by hearing. And as Jesus said, "All things are possible to him that believes." So to get back on track, find out what the Bible says about you, and then give your heart a good talking to.

Are you willing to encourage yourself when you are having a down day or do you need other people to do it for you?

*And David was greatly distressed; for the people spake of stoning him, because the soul of all the people was grieved, every man for his sons and for his daughters: but David encouraged himself in the Lord his God. (1 Samuel 30:6 KJV)*

## We're Not Here by Chance

Suppose you were standing in front of an intricate sand sculpture of the Minneapolis skyline. What would you think if someone told you that the previous night it had been a big pile of sand and a gust of wind had blown through and just happened to shape that sand into the detailed sculpture before you? You would say that it was impossible for such a design to result from random chance. How much more unlikely is it that the wondrously intricate universe is the product of chance? The belief that we are nothing more than a cosmic accident is a false assumption that will keep you from winning in life.

Have you fallen sway to man's opinion about how this world began?

*In the beginning God created the heaven and the earth.* (Genesis 1:1 KJV)

#  Be a Rewarder

Did you know that rewarding people is a God-given idea? Throughout the Bible, we see over and over that God rewards those who are diligent to follow Him. In the same way, you should be quick to reward hard work when you see it. Reward your employees with a bonus or a raise. Bless your kids with something they've wanted for a long time. When you see someone working hard, be quick to notice and reward it in some way. Public recognition and verbal praise don't cost you anything—and it only takes a moment to say, "Thank you" or "Good job." God created us to respond to rewards, so employ it wherever you can. Consistently reward good behavior, and you'll see a consistent good effort in return.

Do you reward your kids, employees or others under your authority in some way when they've consistently done good?

*...The Lord render to every man his righteousness and his faithfulness....*

(1 Samuel 26:23 KJV)

MAY

# 1 God Wants You to Win

Whether it's the Super Bowl, the Olympics, politics, or the stock market, our society has historically placed a high value upon winning. Yet there are those today who think winning is bad. Some have even suggested that kids shouldn't play games in which someone wins because that means someone would lose and feel bad about it! In spite of anything you may have heard to the contrary, most of us have a strong desire to be associated with victory—and that's okay. In fact, God put that desire to win on the inside of each and every one of us. That's why it's so unfortunate when people are taught that winning is unimportant at best and unbiblical at worst. Winning is okay when you do it God's way.

## Have you fallen for the lie that God doesn't want you to win?

*For whatsoever is born of God overcometh the world: and this is the victory that overcometh the world, even our faith. Who is he that overcometh the world, but he that believeth that Jesus is the Son of God?* (1 John 5:4–5 KJV)

#  2   Finish What You Start

Dale Carnegie used to say, "I know men in the ranks who will not stay in the ranks for long. Why? Because they have the ability to get things done." Some people simply know how to get things done. When you're looking for the next generation of leaders in your organization, these types of individuals are a good place to start your search. Find a problem that needs solving and assemble a group of people whose normal responsibilities don't include tackling that problem. The person who grabs hold of the problem and won't let go has leadership potential. This quality is critical in leaders, for at times, nothing but one's iron will says, "Keep going."

> Have you identified the people around you who know how to get things done?

*Now you should finish what you started. Let the eagerness you showed in the beginning be matched now by your giving. Give in proportion to what you have.*
(2 Corinthians 8:11 NLT)

# Go Beyond the Superficial

Four hundred years before the birth of Christ, the famous Greek physician, Hippocrates, made a statement about relationships that still rings with truth today: "Many admire; few know." Hippocrates was pointing out that in his day, as in ours, the vast majority of relationships never get past a superficial level. Often, we don't truly come to know even those who are closest to us. The Bible urges us to stop basing our relationships with others on outward things such as appearance and position but to learn to know the real person, the person on the inside. It's one of God's keys to building winning relationships.

## Are you willing to learn more about the people in your life?

*Wherefore henceforth know we no man after the flesh: yea, though we have known Christ after the flesh, yet now henceforth know we him no more.* (2 Corinthians 5:16 KJV)

# Don't Let Fear Lead You

George Addair once said, "Everything you've ever wanted is on the other side of fear." He was absolutely right. Fear causes us to limit our actions or stop pursuing our dreams because we don't believe success will come. If Walt Disney had allowed fear to rule his life, we would not have Disney as we know it today. You see, he went through multiple business failures before the Walt Disney Corporation found the footing that led to its success. Doubt has killed more dreams than failure ever will, so I encourage you to live in such a way that you empower your dreams, not your fears.

Are you determined to let faith and not fear drive your decisions?

*The fear of man lays a snare, but whoever trusts in the Lord is safe.*
(Proverbs 29:25 ESV)

# 5    Set the Example

Employee manuals and policy handbooks do not create a corporate culture. The atmosphere in a business or a home is most strongly influenced not by what the leader says but by what the leader does. Recognizing the power of setting the right example was one of the leadership secrets of Jesus. When leaders demand punctuality but chronically arrive late for meetings, they send a mixed message that will poison the attitudes of those they are trying to influence.

What kind of "by example" training will the people around you receive today?

*Brethren, be followers together of me, and mark them which walk so as ye have us for an ensample.* (Philippians 3:17 KJV)

#  6 Listen to Others

Every human has an innate need to be heard. We want people to understand our problems, hear our opinions, and sympathize with our pain. If you want a surefire way to win in your relationships, learn to listen well. When talking to other people, ask questions that allow them to talk about themselves. Be genuinely interested in what they have to say. When you do this consistently with the people you meet, peoples' opinions of you will elevate. You'll become an influence in their lives all because you created a conversation and took the time to listen.

Are you truly putting others first
in your conversation?

*Therefore, as God's chosen people, holy and dearly loved, clothe yourselves with compassion, kindness, humility, gentleness and patience. Bear with each other and forgive one another if any of you has a grievance against someone. Forgive as the Lord forgave you. And over all these virtues put on love, which binds them all together in perfect unity.* (Colosssians 3:12–14 NIV)

#  When Winning Doesn't Work

At times, winning an argument may be more harmful than letting the person you disagree with have the last word. You see, by the time you've won an argument, you have possibly damaged a relationship with a friend, spouse, or family member. That broken relationship will leak over into other areas in your life, for as you get used to tension within that relationship going forward, you'll make room for tension in other relationships as well. This is why we must, instead, prioritize people over our opinions. That doesn't mean you let people walk all over you. Identify your personal boundaries and stick with them... and then choose people every other time.

Are you okay placing a priority on your relationships instead of being right?

*Have nothing to do with foolish, ignorant controversies; you know that they breed quarrels. And the Lord's servant must not be quarrelsome but kind to everyone....* (2 Timothy 2:23–24 ESV)

#  8    The Danger of Anger

One of the most corrosive feelings we can have toward other people is anger. We often can come up with a reason for being angry, but that doesn't mean it's right. Benjamin Franklin once said, "Anger is never without a reason, but seldom with a good one." When you feel anger stir up inside you, remember what James 1:20 says: "...man's anger does not promote the righteousness God [wishes and requires]" (Amp.). As Mark Twain said, "Anger is an acid that can do more harm to the vessel in which it is stored than to anything on which it is poured." The person who is damaged the most from your anger is you.

## Have you let anger poison your life?

*Whoever is slow to anger is better than the mighty, and he who rules his spirit than he who takes a city.* (Proverbs 16:32 ESV)

# 9 Seek to Understand

In his bestseller, *The 7 Habits of Highly Effective People*, Stephen Covey writes, "The single most important principle I have learned in the field of interpersonal relationships is this: 'Seek first to understand, then to be understood.'" That principle is a biblical one. In the book of John, we read about Jesus, a Jew, encountering a Samaritan woman. Although much racial and religious hostility existed between their cultures, Jesus was able to cut through her suspicion and anger and exert a profound influence on that woman's life. How? He communicated in love and listened carefully. By doing so, He gave a practical example of the principle: seek to understand before trying to be understood. I encourage you to do the same.

## What is more important to you: understanding others or being understood?

*Happy is the man that findeth wisdom, and the man that getteth understanding. For the merchandise of it is better than the merchandise of silver, and the gain thereof than fine gold.* (Proverbs 3:13–14 KJV)

# True Contentment

A lot of people misunderstand contentment. They wonder, "How can I be content when my marriage is failing? How can I be content when my bills aren't getting paid?" That's when it's important to remember that being content doesn't mean you accept the status quo. When you are content, you know God will never leave you or forsake you. You are happy because you know who you are in Christ. You are filled with inward sufficiency and a certainty that God is more than enough for every situation you face. None of your circumstances, whether negative or positive, can change that. Your happiness lies solely in the Lord. That's a sign that you are walking in true contentment.

## What makes you content?

*Not that I speak in respect of want: for I have learned, in whatsoever state I am, therewith to be content. I know both how to be abased, and I know how to abound: every where and in all things I am instructed both to be full and to be hungry, both to abound and to suffer need.* (Philippians 4:11–12 KJV)

## 11 Appreciate Small Beginnings

We live in a day in which the need for instant gratification has become so strong that few people are willing to start small and grow. The feeling is, "If it can't be instantly huge, why bother?" It's a good thing Jesus didn't think that way. He came to save the world but left it with only 120 committed followers. The book of Zechariah says, "Do not despise the day of small beginnings." Jesus didn't and neither should you.

Is there some area in your life in which you're despising the day of small beginnings?

*For who hath despised the day of small things? for they shall rejoice, and shall see the plummet in the hand of Zerubbabel with those seven; they are the eyes of the Lord, which run to and fro through the whole earth.* (Zechariah 4:10 KJV)

# 12. You Need More Than Truth

Effective communication is the doorway to better relationships, and better relationships are the key to many of the good things life has to offer. One of the best guidelines for good communication is found in Ephesians 4:15. We're encouraged to "speak the truth in love." Truth spoken without love can wound; that's why we talk about someone being "brutally honest." Truthfulness is certainly important, but if you want to enjoy the success and favor that comes from being an outstanding communicator, you're going to have to be more than merely honest. You're going to have to learn to speak the truth in love.

## When you speak, do you season your communication with both truth and love?

*Rather, let our lives lovingly express truth [in all things, speaking truly, dealing truly, living truly]. Enfolded in love, let us grow up in every way and in all things into Him Who is the Head, [even] Christ (the Messiah, the Anointed One).* (Ephesians 4:15 Amp.)

## 13 Lead Without Fear

Many people settle for a level of relational leadership much lower than their potential simply because of fear. They fail to seek new relationships because of fear of rejection or fear of self-disclosure. The great Minnesotan, James F. Bell, founder of General Mills once said, "Fear is an insidious virus. Given a breeding place in our minds, it will permeate the whole body and eat away our spirit and block the forward path of our endeavors." Next time you sense fear trying to grab hold of your heart, turn to God. Let faith in Him drive your life and leadership instead.

Are you allowing fear to block your progress in cultivating relationships and thus block your growth as a leader?

*What time I am afraid, I will trust in thee. In God I will praise his word, in God I have put my trust; I will not fear what flesh can do unto me.* (Psalm 56:3–4 KJV)

## When Hurt Doesn't Justify Offense

It's easy to say, "Don't be offended." It's difficult to put that into practice, particularly when you've been genuinely hurt by someone. Whatever the cause of the offense, it's tempting to stay offended, but you will never find complete success in life when you hold a grudge. Internalizing anger or offense will always affect you the most because it creates an inner turmoil, bitterness, and resentment that is self-destructive. You can choose to move beyond the offense by choosing forgiveness. The apostle Paul tells us that when we act out of love, we choose not to take offense. So always remember that justified hurt never justifies offense. Forgiveness is always your best option.

# Do you justify offense or keep it far from you?

*Then said he unto the disciples, It is impossible but that offences will come: but woe unto him, through whom they come! It were better for him that a millstone were hanged about his neck, and he cast into the sea, than that he should offend one of these little ones. Take heed to yourselves: If thy brother trespass against thee, rebuke him; and if he repent, forgive him. And if he trespass against thee seven times in a day, and seven times in a day turn again to thee, saying, I repent; thou shalt forgive him. And the apostles said unto the Lord, Increase our faith.* (Luke 17:1–5 KJV)

#  Be a Person of Character

You and I are often very good at living other people's lives. We watch them live and critique what they do, usually coming up with a much better way of handling things. We just know that if we were in their shoes, we would have done things much differently—and better. The truth of the matter is that we find it much easier to criticize others than to criticize ourselves. We find plenty of reasons to justify our own mistakes, yet critique those same actions in others. Criticism may make you feel like the better person, but as author Dale Carnegie stated, "Any fool can criticize, condemn, and complain but it takes character and self-control to be understanding and forgiving."

What do people expect from you: criticism, condemnation, or character?

*Do not speak evil against one another, brothers. The one who speaks against a brother or judges his brother, speaks evil against the law and judges the law.* (James 4:11 ESV)

# 16 Go Above Expectations

One of the essential qualifications for the workplace is the habit of performing not merely up to expectations but beyond them. Delivering that kind of performance on a consistent basis is only possible when you possess the quality called commitment. A CEO of a Fortune 500 company wrote, "Essentially there are two actions in life: performance and excuses." George Washington Carver once said, "Ninety-nine percent of failures come from people who have the habit of making excuses." Some people receive a task and run with it. Others run away from it. Commitment is the quality that separates the two and makes you a winner in the workplace.

Are you committed to go above and beyond what is expected of you at your workplace?

*So, whether you eat or drink, or whatever you do, do all to the glory of God.*
(1 Corinthians 10:31 ESV)

Be Open With Others

Are you a trust builder? I hope so. It's vital to your success. If people don't trust you, they'll never open their lives to your influence. To influence others in a godly manner, you must learn the art of self-disclosure. People must know what's truly in your heart before they can be sure you're someone they can trust. God Himself has been our example in this. Throughout the Bible, He willingly disclosed His heart so His people could learn to trust Him. Influence can't occur without trust— and trust can't occur without a careful measure of self-disclosure.

Will you dare to be more open with those around you today?

*Keep open house; be generous with your lives. By opening up to others, you'll prompt people to open up with God, this generous Father in heaven.* (Matthew 5:16 Msg.)

## 18  First Impressions

When you and I meet new people, we often make quick decisions about who they are based on their appearance and demeanor. The prophet Samuel did this. God brought him to David's family to anoint a king over Israel. Samuel assumed that the handsome Eliab, David's oldest brother, was the person God wanted to anoint. But God had someone else picked out. First Samuel 16:7 says, "God does not see the same way people see. People look at the outside of a person, but the Lord looks at the heart." It wasn't until Samuel met David, an unassuming teenager, that God told him to anoint Israel's next king. Next time you meet someone, realize that you don't know his whole story. God does, and He may use that relationship to bring His blessing into your life.

What do you expect when you make a new acquaintance: a fleeting moment or a potential divine appointment?

*Look beneath the surface so you can judge correctly.* (John 7:24 NLT)

# 19 Don't Rush Into God's Plan

After reading 1 Samuel 16:13, you may assume that David became king within days, weeks, or even months from being anointed by the prophet Samuel, but that wasn't the case. It was conservatively around 15 years before he actually became king in Israel. During that time spent waiting, David could easily have flaunted the fact that Samuel anointed him king, or he could have attempted to make himself king much earlier. When Saul was hunting David down with the intent to kill him, David had more than one opportunity to kill Saul. Instead of "helping" God's plan along, he stated, "The Lord forbid that I should stretch forth mine hand against the Lord's anointed." David chose to honor King Saul and wait for God to move him into position.

## Have you ever tried to make God's plans happen before He did?

*Then Samuel took the horn of oil, and anointed him in the midst of his brethren: and the Spirit of the Lord came upon David from that day forward..."*
(1 Samuel 16:13 KJV)

# 20  Keep Learning

Some people think the educational process ended the day they graduated from school. Others make learning a lifelong quest. Guess which group tends to experience more happiness and success on the job? Proverbs 1:5 says, "A wise man will increase learning." If you want to be happier in your present job and increase your chances of getting a better one, make a commitment to learn everything you can about your current field. People who are chronically unhappy on the job tend to be those who only want to get by doing the bare minimum. They never try to learn more about their vocation. If you want happiness and promotion on the job, follow the Bible's advice—grow in knowledge about your position.

## What can you do to learn more about your current job?

*Intelligent people are always ready to learn. Their ears are open for knowledge.* (Proverbs 18:15 NLT)

#  21   Enthusiastic Leadership

Great dreams can generate incredible energy, but only when shared in inspiring ways. Effective leaders go beyond clarity. Their vision is wrapped in enthusiasm, conviction, and sincerity. They consistently convey an optimism that labels themselves and others as winners despite all odds. This kind of leadership is an especially crucial quality in times of organizational stress. In a moment of great crisis, Jesus of Nazareth told His followers, "Don't let your hearts be troubled. Believe in me." He moved them from fear to hope with His inspiring leadership.

## What kind of energy do you bring to those around you?

*Don't let your hearts be troubled. Trust in God, and trust also in me. There is more than enough room in my Father's home. If this were not so, would I have told you that I am going to prepare a place for you? When everything is ready, I will come and get you, so that you will always be with me where I am. And you know the way to where I am going.* (John 14:1–4 NLT)

# Forgiveness Includes Forgetting

When someone has hurt you, it's not easy to forgive them. In fact, it often seems easier—and much more gratifying—to sit and stew over how they've wronged you. What people don't realize, though, is that forgiveness is for your benefit just as much—if not more—as it is for the person who hurt you. Author Lewis Smedes put it this way: "To forgive is to set a prisoner free and discover that the prisoner was you." When you continually choose to hold a grudge, that unforgiveness holds you captive to frustration and anger. You will be filled with unrest until you allow yourself to forgive. That's why the Bible tells us time and again: forgive and forget, just as the Lord forgives you.

## Is baggage from the past weighing down the future of your relationships?

*For if ye forgive men their trespasses, your heavenly Father will also forgive you: But if ye forgive not men their trespasses, neither will your Father forgive your trespasses.* (Matthew 6:14–15 KJV)

Something Larger Than You

History has consistently shown that people are hungry to live their lives for something larger than themselves. Leaders who offer it will have no shortage of followers. In fact, the need for a higher purpose is so basic to the human soul, the Bible says, "Where there is no vision the people perish." Jesus modeled a leadership style that gave people this larger, grander vision. Numerous studies have shown that people will work harder, longer, and better when they understand the significance of their individual contributions.

Do you help others understand the significance of what they do?

*Ye have not chosen me, but I have chosen you, and ordained you, that ye should go and bring forth fruit, and that your fruit should remain: that whatsoever ye shall ask of the Father in my name, He may give it to you.* (John 15:16 KJV)

## 24 The Importance of Respect

Since the 1992 U.S. men's Olympic basketball team could include NBA players, it was unofficially named the "Dream Team." The roster included everyone from Michael Jordan to Larry Bird and Patrick Ewing. With all those great team members, the coaching staff had an interesting task: what could they teach these basketball superstars? Head coach Chuck Daly knew. In their first meeting, he told the players that the most important thing for them to do was to be on time. If they showed up late, they showed a lack of respect for their teammates. Michael Jordan set the stage the next day when he showed up 45 minutes early. He knew what Coach Daly knew: respect is key to success in your relationships.

### Is respect evident in your relationships?

*Love one another with brotherly affection. Outdo one another in showing honor.* (Romans 12:10 ESV)

#  25   A Valuable Employee

I once heard the anatomy of an organization described like this: The wishbones are the people who sit around wishing so-and-so wasn't their boss and that things were different than the way they currently were. The jawbones can "spin a good yarn," but people purposely avoid them during the day because they talk your ear off and waste your time. The knucklebones knock everything that happens with criticism. Then there are the backbones. These are the people you can always lean on because they support the organization with quiet, effective, and unassuming behavior. These are the people who have multiple qualities of a valuable employee.

## Which employee are you?

*Lazy people want much but get little, but those who work hard will prosper.*
(Proverbs 13:4 NLT)

# 26 The Trap of Pride

Hollywood loves to portray business executives and other successful people as arrogant and rude. It's an unfair stereotype, but it's accurate more often than it should be. The truth is, when you experience some success, it's easy to fall into the trap of pride. One of the Bible's keys to growing an organization is maintaining a humble spirit. Don't fall into the trap of arrogance. Not only is it unseemly, it's bad business. In the book of Isaiah we read, "The arrogance of a man will be brought low and the pride of men humbled."

## Have you fallen into the trap of pride?

*When pride cometh, then cometh shame: but with the lowly is wisdom.*
(Proverbs 11:2 KJV)

# Why Do You Work?

Do you know your job can be more to you than a way to earn money? When you are focused on the fact that your job brings you a paycheck, it can be easy to get worn out at work. When you change your perspective, though, you'll find a good reason to go to work, and that reason is people. Anytime you look outside of yourself and focus on those around you, you'll find your job will become much less stressful and more enjoyable. Even if it is as simple as encouraging a coworker or being nice to a customer, understanding the big picture of how you are impacting lives through your work will change your job from a necessity to privilege.

## How can you impact people through your job?

*I am crucified with Christ: nevertheless I live; yet not I, but Christ liveth in me: and the life which I now live in the flesh I live by the faith of the Son of God, who loved me, and gave himself for me.* (Galatians 2:20 KJV)

# 28 Why Are You Here?

One of the great industrialists of the last century, George Eberhard, once stated, "The vital force in business life is the honest desire to serve. Business, it is said, is the science of service. He profits most who serves best." That truth is at the heart of Jesus' declaration that "He that would be the greatest among you must be the servant of all." All lasting leadership begins with servanthood. If things are not going well with you, examine the level of service you are rendering to others and the spirit with which you are delivering it. As you strive to meet the needs of others, you'll find your influence growing.

> Are you more interested in serving or in being served?

*But this is not your calling. You will lead by a different model. The greatest one among you will live as one called to serve others without honor. The greatest honor and authority is reserved for the one who has a servant heart.* (Luke 22:26 TPT)

**29** Who Are You Behind Closed Doors?

The great evangelist Dwight L. Moody once said, "Character is what you are in the dark." One of the major differences between those who have a form of success and those who truly win in every area of life is character. It's possible to lie, cheat, and steal your way into a form of prosperity, but it's an empty and fleeting type of success. You can't build a winning life without strong personal character. That means being the kind of person who does the right thing when doing the right thing is the hardest thing to do. The rewards of strong character are great. Proverbs 2:7 says God is a shield to those who walk in integrity. Character. It's one of the identifying marks of a winner.

How strong is your shield of character?

*We can rejoice, too, when we run into problems and trials, for we know that they help us develop endurance. And endurance develops strength of character, and character strengthens our confident hope of salvation. (Romans 5:3–4 NLT)*

# 30  Stay Motivated

The world is moved by highly motivated people: men and women who want something very much, believe very much, and inspire those around them to believe along with them. It's one thing for you to keep yourself personally motivated to achieve excellence on the job, but it's another to have the ability to impart that kind of motivation to those around you. Few things cause you to stand out and make you more valuable to an organization than being the kind of person who inspires your coworkers to go higher and further. That kind of infectious enthusiasm is one of the top attributes that will make you a standout on the job.

## Are you motivated to work hard on the job?

*And let us consider how we may spur one another on toward love and good deeds, not giving up meeting together, as some are in the habit of doing, but encouraging one another —and all the more as you see the Day approaching.* (Hebrews 10:24–25 NIV)

# What Is Your Plan?

A deep commitment to a sound plan and a firm determination to carry it out is a foundational truth for both individuals and organizations. Without a plan, you have nowhere to go and nothing toward which to direct your energies. Without a plan, you can only react to circumstances. That's why careful planning is one of the Bible's keys to organizational increase. As we read in Proverbs 21:5, "The plans of the diligent lead surely to advantage, but everyone who is hasty comes surely to poverty."

> Are you being hasty or are you pursuing a plan with determination?

*Commit your actions to the Lord, and your plans will succeed.* (Proverbs 16:3 NLT)

JUNE

Image • Eastman Childs

#  Defeat Complacency

One of the greatest enemies of growth a business will face comes after it has experienced some success. It is the enemy of complacency. It is altogether too easy to achieve something and then rest upon your achievements—but this lack of action will cause you to lose momentum. One of Martin Luther King Jr.'s mentors, Benjamin Mays, put it this way: "The tragedy of life is often not in our failure, but rather in our complacency; not in our doing too much, but rather in our doing too little; not in our living above our ability, but rather in our living below our capacities."

### Are you pressing higher or resting on your laurels?

*For the waywardness of the simple will kill them, and the complacency of fools will destroy them....* (Proverbs 1:32 NIV)

## 2 What's Your Motive?

No matter who you are, your ability to establish healthy relationships is vital to your happiness and growth. To build relationships that last, you must establish them on a solid foundation. The good news is that the Bible gives us some practical keys to laying that kind of firm foundation. One of those keys is unselfish motives. Take an honest look inside yourself. Are you pursuing relationships based on selfish motives? If so, you are building them on a shaky base. Proverbs 16:2 says, "All a man's ways seem innocent to him, but motives are weighed by the Lord." Seek the best interests of others and your relationships will be off to a great start.

Are you keeping your relationships centered on you or on other people?

*Every way of a man is right in his own eyes, but the Lord weighs and tries the hearts.* (Proverbs 21:2 Amp.)

# 3 Be Confident in Him

There is a level of confidence that comes from a relationship with God that some people may interpret as recklessness. But with this divine boldness comes the ability to accomplish great and wonderful things. Proverbs 3:26 says, "For the Lord will be your confidence and will keep your foot from being caught." The Hebrew word translated "confidence" comes from a root word that means "foolish." Some people consider bold action foolishness and mistake confidence for arrogance. That's what happened when young David chose to take on a giant named Goliath—and you know how that story ended.

## Do you have this kind of confidence?

*Not that we are sufficient of ourselves to think any thing as of ourselves; but our sufficiency is of God;* (2 Corinthians 3:5 KJV)

# 4 Be Productive

Are you a time thief? People who would never consider stealing money or merchandise, steal something just as valuable every day. They steal time from their employers. For most, a job is a transaction. Your employer agrees to pay you a certain amount of money in exchange for a certain number of hours of productivity. When you accept payment for time spent doing anything else, you're a time thief. What most don't realize is that making a practice of stealing time puts spiritual laws in motion that make it hard for you to experience real happiness on the job. Ephesians 5:16 says, "Be wise and make the most of your time." It's another key to staying happy on the job.

When you are on the job,
are you giving your all?

*Training us to renounce ungodliness and worldly passions, and to live self-controlled, upright, and godly lives in the present age....* (Titus 2:12 ESV)

# 5   What Are You Really Saying?

We've all been in a conversation with people whose arms are crossed, they've started to yawn, and they're continually looking at the clock. Their nonverbal signals communicate they aren't listening to what you are saying. Ralph Waldo Emerson once said, "When the eyes say one thing, and the tongue another, a practiced man relies on the language of the first." Good nonverbal communication includes an open posture, eye contact, and nodding in response to the other person. So when listening to others speak, make a point to ensure your nonverbal communication is engaged with your current conversation.

Do you recognize what signals you are sending nonverbally during a conversation?

*[Let your] love be sincere (a real thing); hate what is evil [loathe all ungodliness, turn in horror from wickedness], but hold fast to that which is good.*
(Romans 12:9 Amp.)

# 6 Don't Murmur

Some leaders really shine when the battle is on, but when the pressure is off, they lose effectiveness. Are you that type of leader? You can tell by listening carefully to what you say. Challenges can bring out the best in you and make you an inspiration to yourself and others. But how do you respond to day-to-day drudgery? Do you moan and complain like everyone else? Negative words are a fast-spreading poison. They are a luxury a leader simply cannot afford. The Bible calls it murmuring and has some strong warnings against it.

> When things are in a lull, do you stay enthusiastic and encourage others to do the same?

*Neither murmur ye, as some of them also murmured, and were destroyed of the destroyer.* (1 Corinthians 10:10 KJV)

#  Quiet May Be Best

Today's society often equates bigger, faster, and louder with better. The problem is, many people unknowingly carry this expectation over into their expectations about God. They expect a loud voice from heaven or an over-the-top miracle to answer their prayers. God can do both of these things, but more often than not, His leading is quiet. Elijah discovered this in 1 Kings 19. God's voice wasn't in the strong wind that broke rocks into pieces. He didn't talk through the earthquake or fire. It was only after these things subsided that Elijah heard God's still, small voice. If you want to get to know God better, listen to the psalmist's words in Psalm 46:10: "Be still and know that I am God."

*And he said, Go forth, and stand upon the mount before the Lord. And, behold, the Lord passed by, and a great and strong wind rent the mountains, and brake in pieces the rocks before the Lord; but the Lord was not in the wind: and after the wind an earthquake; but the Lord was not in the earthquake: and after the earthquake a fire; but the Lord was not in the fire: and after the fire a still small voice.* (1 Kings 19:11–12 KJV)

Are you spending time away from the noise of life to listen to the Lord?

#  Make Room for Honesty

A realtor once pointed out that one frustrating aspect of his job is that most people like the concept of honesty, but not the practice of it. They want realtors to be honest, but respond negatively when their agent doesn't agree with what they think. It's a good reminder that honesty is only possible when you provide a safe environment for someone to disagree with you. Use a conflict of interest as a launching pad for a well-balanced discussion, not an attack on the other person. The world wasn't created to be puppets of each other, but unique, honest individuals. So remember, disagreement should not be a signal for dislike, rather a nod to a different opinion that could benefit your own.

## Do you allow other people to be honest?

*Better is a poor person who walks in his integrity than one who is crooked in speech and is a fool.* (Proverbs 19:1 ESV)

# 9  The Foundation of Self-Control

You've wrestled with that bad habit for years, but now you've decided to deal with it once and for all and there's no turning back. Congratulations! You've just discovered the first key to self-control. Your first step in overcoming any habit or destructive behavior pattern is to make a quality decision—or you could say, an unwavering commitment—to master it. That may sound simple, but it's true. Resolve is the very foundation of self-control. Without it, your efforts will ultimately fail. The Bible says that a double-minded man is unstable in all he does. So don't vacillate or make a half-hearted decision; count the cost, set your will, and make a quality decision.

## Will you make a quality decision to master your bad habits?

*But I discipline my body and keep it under control, lest after preaching to others I myself should be disqualified.* (1 Corinthians 9:27 ESV)

**Vision Creates Passion**

To be an effective leader, you must be a visionary. Visionaries boldly appeal to anyone and everyone to get on board with the vision. They talk about it, write about it, and burn white-hot for it. They are future-oriented and full of faith to believe the vision can be achieved if the dream is pressed toward with enough desire. If told their dream is impossible, that just adds fuel to the fire in their spirit. They carry the vision. They cast the vision. They draw people into the vision, and they'll give their lives to see it fulfilled.

Do you have a God-given vision, and if so, how passionately are you pursuing it?

*Where there is no vision, the people perish: but he that keepeth the law, happy is he.* (Proverbs 29:18 KJV)

## 11  Lead With Loyalty

In the realms of leadership, achievement, and organizational increase, there is one element that is worth its weight in gold. That rare element is loyalty. Loyalty cannot be blueprinted. It cannot be produced on an assembly line. In fact, it cannot be artificially formulated at all because its origin is the human heart. It grows there only when it has been planted there. As the Bible says, like begets like, and we reap only what we sow. Loyalty can't be demanded. It can only be earned. If you want those you lead to be loyal to you and to your vision, you must be loyal to them.

Are you sowing loyalty into those you are charged with leading?

*Loyalty makes a person attractive. It is better to be poor than dishonest.* (Proverbs 19:22 NLT)

# God Uses Imperfect People

Did you know that you don't have to be perfect before God can use you? Take a look at some of the men and women of faith we read about in the Bible. You'll quickly see that none of them were perfect. Abraham lied, yet later became the father of our faith. Rahab was a prostitute who ended up in the lineage of Jesus. David committed adultery, yet God still called him a man after His own heart. Paul oversaw the killing of Christians and later went on to write over two-thirds of the New Testament. The list could go on. God uses imperfect people who repent of their sins and turn their lives over to Christ. Don't ever let the Devil tell you that your past failures will hold you back in life. God accepts you just as you are.

> Do you realize that God accepts you, flaws and all?

*But if we confess our sins to him, he is faithful and just to forgive us our sins and to cleanse us from all wickedness.* (1 John 1:9 NLT)

# 13 Compel Each Other

King Solomon, known for his great wisdom, wrote this truth in Ecclesiastes: "Two are better than one; because if they fall, the one will lift up his fellow: but woe to him that is alone when he falleth; for he hath not another to help him up." Solomon observed that two are better than one, because if one falls, the other is there to encourage and exhort the other to get up and carry on. That's what couples in winning marriages do. They "compel" each other on to excellence.

> Are you a good influence
> in your spouse's life?

*You use steel to sharpen steel, and one friend sharpens another.*
(Proverbs 27:17 Msg.)

# 14 Innovate

One of the most valuable traits any leader can possess is the ability to innovate. Innovation is the ability to create effective new ways to get the job done. Innovators never stop learning and growing. They find new solutions to problems, new ways to deal with changing circumstances, and fresh ways to accomplish the organization's mission. Most innovators move against the tide of majority opinion, which usually resists change. That's why innovators must possess the confidence to move ahead despite opposition.

## Do you have the courage to innovate?

*For we are his workmanship, created in Christ Jesus unto good works, which God hath before ordained that we should walk in them.* (Ephesians 2:10 KJV)

# 15 Assemble a Team

Once Jesus began His ministry, He wasted no time in beginning to assemble a team. He handpicked individuals from a variety of backgrounds, often with the simple call, "Follow me." Jesus' mission was to save the world, but He chose not to do it alone. If you want to accomplish something significant, one of the most basic steps toward attainment of your goal is to form a team. Few one-man-bands ever achieve greatness.

> What are you trying to do alone that a team would help you accomplish?

*And Jesus, walking by the sea of Galilee, saw two brethren, Simon called Peter, and Andrew his brother, casting a net into the sea: for they were fishers. And he saith unto them, Follow me, and I will make you fishers of men.* (Matthew 4:18–19 KJV)

# 16  The Right Risks

Charles Lindbergh once said, "All glory comes from daring to begin." The willingness to take reasonable risks is one of the attributes wise leaders look for in those they raise to positions of leadership. If you want to position yourself for promotion and increase, you'll need to be a person of action... someone who makes things happen. Georges Clemenceau once said, "A man who has to be convinced to act before he acts is not a man of action." Being a person of action—someone willing to take calculated, reasonable risks—is one of the attributes that can make you a star at work.

Are you willing to take calculated risks on the job?

*Cast thy bread upon the waters: for thou shalt find it after many days.*
(Ecclesiastes 11:1 KJV)

## Listen Beyond the Delivery

Are you missing important messages because of the messenger's style? Here is one of the recommendations that came out of a study on the keys to effective listening: "Judge what the speaker says, not how it is said." In other words, don't let a speaker's delivery get in the way of your understanding a message. An angry messenger may have some valuable insight. Tune out an angry speaker and you may miss a priceless nugget of information.

### Can you look past the messenger's delivery for insight?

*If you readily receive correction, you are walking on the path to life. But if you reject rebuke, you're guaranteed to go astray.* (Proverbs 10:17 TPT)

# 18   Cherish Your Marriage

If you had to make a list of the most precious things you possess, where on that list would we find your marriage? Some in our culture today don't think marriage is a precious possession, but those who have outstanding marriages do. One habit of happily married people is that they cherish each other. Start seeing your relationship with your spouse as a precious thing, then begin nourishing and cherishing it. It will change your marriage.

> Does your spouse see your actions and know you cherish your marriage?

*As the Scriptures say, "A man leaves his father and mother and is joined to his wife, and the two are united into one." This is a great mystery, but it is an illustration of the way Christ and the church are one.*
(Ephesians 5:31–32 NLT)

# 19 Be Transparent

Does being a leader mean never allowing anyone to see your mistakes, weaknesses, or fallibilities? Many people seem to think so, but one of the leadership secrets of Jesus was His willingness to be transparent before His disciples. The fact is, Jesus was the first perfect person to ever walk the earth; the people you're trying to lead don't expect you to be the second one. A willingness to engage in some self-disclosure creates an atmosphere of trust and honesty.

## What are the obstacles keeping you from being a more transparent leader?

*Righteous lips are the delight of kings; and they love him that speaketh right.*
(Proverbs 16:13 KJV)

## What's Your Work Ethic?

Would your work habits change significantly if your employer were almighty God, the Creator of the universe? Having God for a boss may strike you as a strange concept, but according to the Bible, that's precisely how we are to approach our jobs. In the book of Ephesians chapter five, we read, "Serve wholeheartedly, as if you were serving the Lord, not men." If God were your boss, would you give only a half-hearted effort? Would you lie, cheat, or steal on the job? Would you criticize or belittle the boss or your coworkers? Probably not. If you'll bring that kind of work ethic to your job and serve God first, you'll soon find that your relationships are more pleasant and your work more rewarding.

## Would God be pleased with your work?

*Servants, be obedient to them that are your masters according to the flesh, with fear and trembling, in singleness of your heart, as unto Christ; not with eyeservice, as menpleasers; but as the servants of Christ, doing the will of God from the heart; with good will doing service, as to the Lord, and not to men:* (Ephesians 6:5–7 KJV)

## 21 Go Beyond Failure

We often think that successful people never face failure, but that's not the case. When General Douglas MacArthur applied for admission to West Point, he was turned down twice before being accepted. Elvis Presley was fired after one performance in 1954 and told he should go back to driving a truck. Beethoven's violin teacher called him hopeless as a composer. Margaret Mitchell's classic book, *Gone With the Wind*, was turned down by more than twenty-five publishers. An expert told Vince Lombardi that he possessed minimal football knowledge and lacked motivation. These stories are just a few of the many examples we have today of people who didn't give up. Failure doesn't determine your success in life. It's what you do after you fail that does.

When you're faced with failure, do you give up or try again?

*And as for you, brethren, do not become weary or lose heart in doing right [but continue in well-doing without weakening].* (2 Thessalonians 3:13 Amp.)

# Timely Words

Have you ever known someone who always seemed to say just the right thing at just the right time? Mark Twain once said, "The difference between the almost right word and the right word is really a large matter—it's the difference between a lightning bug and lightning." If you want to be a person who makes an impact on the people around you, it's important to know what to say and when to say it. The good news is, God wants to help you do just that. Isaiah 50:4 says, "The Lord God hath given me the tongue of the learned, that I should know how to speak a word in season to him that is weary." Wouldn't it be wonderful to be known as a person who brings refreshment and healing with a single, timely word? You can.

## What words are coming out of your mouth?

*Preach the word; be ready in season and out of season; reprove, rebuke, and exhort, with complete patience and teaching.* (2 Timothy 4:2 ESV)

# 23 You Are a Manager

Although the terms are often used interchangeably, there is an important difference between leadership and management. Being a good manager doesn't necessarily make you a good leader—but every good leader should be a competent manager. You may be a one-person operation, but you still must manage your time, your resources, and your relationships. Your skill at managing these three areas largely determines the level of success you will experience in this life.

How are you managing the vital resources that have been entrusted to you?

*Let a man so account of us, as of the ministers of Christ, and stewards of the mysteries of God. Moreover it is required in stewards, that a man be found faithful.* (1 Corinthians 4:1–2 KJV)

**Speak to the Heart and Head**

Would you like to communicate in a way that makes things happen? It's crucial if you want to influence others. To get others to take action, your conversation should have two goals: to motivate and give direction. If you simply inspire people, they may get excited but won't know which way to go. On the other hand, mere instructions probably won't stir them to follow your lead. Combine the two and people move forward. This means you must speak to their heads and their hearts. That's the very reason the Bible is so effective. It's full of practical direction and inspiration. So, to be a more effective leader, do what God does. Speak to the heart and the head for maximum results.

Do you include both motivation and direction when speaking to those under your authority?

*Give me now wisdom and knowledge to go out and come in before this people, for who can rule this Your people who are so great?* (2 Chronicles 1:10 Amp.)

# Build and Rebuild

Have you ever noticed how some people consistently tear you down, while others seem to have the ability to build you up? When you've been built up, you've experienced something the Bible calls "edification." Edification is a fancy-sounding Bible word, but it comes from a Greek word that simply means to rebuild that which has been torn down. In 1 Thessalonians 5:11, we're encouraged to "edify one another." As you encounter others today, your words are going to be used to either tear them down or build them up. Let me encourage you to make a quality decision right now to be a person who is known by those around you as an "edifier."

## Are the words you speak edifying to others?

*And let us consider one another to provoke unto love and to good works: Not forsaking the assembling of ourselves together, as the manner of some is; but exhorting one another: and so much the more, as ye see the day approaching.* (Hebrews 10:24–25 KJV)

#  Your Support System

Have you ever felt as if your friends left you hanging out to dry? Have loved ones ever let you down just when you needed them the most? At those times, what you were looking for was "support." Well, in 2 Chronicles chapter 16, we discover a source of support that can never fail. It says, "For the eyes of the Lord move to and fro throughout the earth that He may strongly support those whose hearts are completely His." The Hebrew word translated "support" means to strengthen, encourage, and protect. God is constantly on the look out to support those who are His.

> Have you looked to the Lord to support you in this life?

*He that dwelleth in the secret place of the most High shall abide under the shadow of the Almighty. I will say of the Lord, He is my refuge and my fortress: my God; in him will I trust.* (Psalm 91:1–2 KJV)

# 27 When a Friend Gets Promoted

An ancient Greek playwright named Aeschylus once wrote, "It is in the character of very few men to honor without envy a friend who has prospered." One key to winning in relationships is learning how to be happy when someone else is honored before you. Our instinct is to be envious or jealous that we didn't get what they did, but both envy and jealousy will destroy your life. Romans 12:15 says we should "rejoice with those who rejoice, and weep with those who weep." Everybody will be blessed and honored at some point in life; your time will come. Until then, choose to be genuinely happy for other people when they encounter good things. They are excited about their new opportunities just as you would be if it happened to you.

## How do you respond when someone else gets promoted in life before you do?

*If one part suffers, all the parts suffer with it, and if one part is honored, all the parts are glad. All of you together are Christ's body, and each of you is a part of it.* (1 Corinthians 12:26–27 NLT)

# Don't Let Envy Sidetrack You

Many people get sidetracked by envy. Envy makes you believe that other people have a better life than you. Envy lures you to think that your life will only be good when it looks different than what you have. Envy misidentifies other people's stories as your best truth. However, none of this is actual truth. You will only be best when you focus on the life you have been given and pursue your dreams. The philosopher Epicurus put it this way: "Do not spoil what you have by desiring what you do not have. Remember that what you now have was once among the things you only hoped for." Envy will tear you apart mentality. Work, instead, to be content.

## Have you let envy seep into your heart?

*Resentment kills a fool, and envy slays the simple.* (Job 5:2 NIV)

## 29 Inspire Others

In the early, difficult days of Federal Express, founder Fred Smith faced a wall of obstacles. Thirty million dollars in debt and sued by his own family, he nearly lost his job as chairman. Yet he inspired such loyalty among his employees that his van drivers pawned their watches to buy gasoline so they could get their packages to the airport on time. Effective leaders have inspirational qualities that motivate common people to do uncommon things. Inspiration is the ability to express vision in ways that move others toward powerful actions.

What are you inspiring people around you to do?

*And let us consider one another to provoke unto love and to good works:* (Hebrews 10:24 KJV)

# Circumstances Can Change

Colonel Sanders appeared to be headed in the wrong direction as he tried to sell his chicken recipe to over 1,000 places and nobody wanted it. Everything changed the day he found a buyer for his recipe. As you well know, his Kentucky Fried Chicken restaurant became much more than I am sure he ever imagined. What a great reminder that no matter what you are facing right now, your life can change for the better. Things don't have to keep going the way they have in the past. This doesn't have to be as good as it gets. No matter who you are and no matter what circumstances you're facing today, together you and God can start turning things around.

> Do you realize that what seems impossible to you is possible with God?

*But Jesus beheld them, and said unto them, With men this is impossible; but with God all things are possible.* (Matthew 19:26 KJV)

JULY

Image • Eastman Childs

#  Use Your Knowledge

The saying that knowledge is power is not quite true. The fact is, "utilized" knowledge is power. And whoever said, "What you don't know can't hurt you," never owned a business. In the book of Proverbs, King Solomon urges us strongly to acquire knowledge, wisdom, and understanding. He called it a "key of life" and "more precious than gold or silver." The great economist J.M. Clark called knowledge, "the only instrument of production that is not subject to diminishing returns." It's the knowledge you wisely put to work that is power.

## Have you been growing in knowledge and using what you know?

*Get all the advice and instruction you can, so you will be wise the rest of your life.*
(Proverbs 19:20 NLT)

## 2  Be Patient

The bamboo tree is one of the most unique plants on earth. When planted as a bulb, all its growth for the first four years occurs entirely underground. For four long years, there are no apparent signs of growth. But in its fifth year, it breaks through the ground and grows up to eighty feet! Sometimes following God's principles of success is like that. You may be doing everything right but see no visible results. That's when it's vital to remember the advice of Galatians 6:9 which says, "Let us not become weary in doing good, for at the proper time, we will reap a harvest if we do not give up." Have you been thinking of giving up? Don't. Patience is an identifying mark of a winner.

Will you remain patient even in the middle of difficulty?

*But let patience have her perfect work, that ye may be perfect and entire, wanting nothing.* (James 1:4 KJV)

# ③ Exemplify Quality

King Solomon said, "Show me a man skilled in his work and I'll show you a man who will stand before kings." Nothing has changed in the last three thousand years. Quality still matters. Andrew Carnegie said, "Quality is never an accident. It is always the result of high intention, sincere effort, intelligent direction, and skillful execution." I would add one more item to Carnegie's list. Quality is always the result of leadership. The commitment to it comes from the top. People may forget how fast you did a job, but they won't forget how well you did it.

> Are you exerting leadership that produces quality in your organization?

*Every man's work shall be made manifest: for the day shall declare it, because it shall be revealed by fire; and the fire shall try every man's work of what sort it is.* (1 Corinthians 3:13 KJV)

True Liberty

Over 200 years ago today, a document we call The Declaration of Independence became the birth certificate of our nation. Today, the highest ideals expressed in that document are in danger of being swept aside in a rising tide of secularism. The signers of the Declaration put their lives on the line when they affirmed a belief that God endows all men with "certain unalienable" rights. Today, such talk of a Creator or a divine origin for values and truth is not welcome in the public square. Whereas the founding fathers fought for freedom "of" religion, some today demand freedom "from" religion. They have forgotten what the signers of the Declaration knew all too well. Without God, there is no true liberty.

Are you walking in the freedom only God can bring you?

*If the Son therefore shall make you free, ye shall be free indeed.* (John 8:36 KJV)

# 5 Be Faithful

We're living in an age in which people find it increasingly difficult to trust. Skepticism and cynicism are hallmarks of our approach to relationships. It is possible to increase your level of positive influence on the people around you—but influence only grows in an atmosphere of trust. And in these cautious, suspicious days in which we live, winning someone's trust is harder than ever. It can be done, however, if you do what the Bible in Psalm 37:3 calls "cultivating faithfulness." That means being known by others as a person of integrity, honesty, and compassion. When you cultivate faithfulness in your relationships, your opportunities for positive influence will grow.

## What are you cultivating in your relationships?

*Trust in the Lord and do good; dwell in the land and cultivate faithfulness.*
(Psalm 37:3 NASB)

# 6  What Are You Majoring in?

I see it all the time—parents who have fallen into the trap of majoring on the minors in the lives of their children and thus neglecting the more important things. A red herring is a trivial matter blown up to seem important in order to get you to ignore that which truly is significant. Where your children are concerned, red herrings get you so interested in peripheral things that you expend all your parental capital and energy trying to exert your will on the matter. Then the really big issues—the ones with long-term implications for the health and success of your child—often go unaddressed.

Are you spending all your energy parenting red herrings?

*Lo, children are an heritage of the Lord: and the fruit of the womb is his reward.*
(Psalm 127:3 KJV)

# Let Faith Win

Two forces are constantly at work in this world: faith and fear. One will bring you peace. The other will bring uncertainty and worry. In fact, the very presence of fear enhances the intensity of any difficulty, pain, or adversity you face. President Franklin Roosevelt once said, "The only thing we have to fear is fear itself." His wife, Eleanor, also understood the battle with fear. She said, "You gain strength, courage, and confidence by every experience in which you really stop to look fear in the face. You must do the thing which you think you cannot do." Overcoming fear should be a priority for each one of us.

Do you have the courage to live a life free from fear?

*Fear not, for I am with you; be not dismayed, for I am your God; I will strengthen you, I will help you, I will uphold you with my righteous right hand.*
(Isaiah 41:10 ESV)

# 8 Work With Excellence

The world is filled with people who are prepared to do no more than the absolute minimum necessary to get by. Do you want to be happy in your work? Do you want to experience promotion and financial reward? If so, you're going to have to consistently do more than is expected of you; get more done than is required; and bring more excellence to your work than the minimum standards demand. This is what Jesus meant when He said, "If someone compels you to go one mile, go with him two miles." That's where we get the phrase, "going the extra mile." Jesus taught us to exceed the expectations of those we work for. It's an important key to finding happiness on the job.

### Do you go "above and beyond" what is required of you?

*And whatsoever ye do, do it heartily, as to the Lord, and not unto men; knowing that of the Lord ye shall receive the reward of the inheritance: for ye serve the Lord Christ.* (Colossians 3:23–24 KJV)

# Be Diligent

Some people just always seem to make things happen. Others seemingly have to be prodded at every turn. Guess which type is most often tapped for leadership and promotion? When you examine the lives of those who rise to positions of responsibility, you will find some common characteristics. And though they are often unaware of it, these individuals are following principles laid down in the Bible. When leaders look to raise up new leaders, they look for people of action—people who simply make things happen—proactive, self-starting individuals who deliver results. The book of Proverbs calls it "boldness and diligence," and it is one characteristic of a star at work.

When on the job, are you diligent to complete the tasks you've been given?

*He becometh poor that dealeth with a slack hand: but the hand of the diligent maketh rich. (Proverbs 10:4 KJV)*

# 10 How to Argue Well

Have you ever noticed how quickly arguments can escalate? You and your spouse start off disagreeing about household chores and somehow end up questioning your love for one another. What probably happened was that somewhere in the middle of that argument you or your spouse let your emotions get the best of you. As some people say, you didn't fight fair. Marriage counselors see this happen quite often when one spouse uses an issue that had already been forgiven as fuel for a current disagreement. Instead of hurting your partner in this way, when you have a disagreement, keep the past behind you so you can focus on the issue at hand. You'll keep forgiveness at the forefront and arrive at a resolution much quicker.

When you disagree, do you keep the past behind you?

*A fool gives full vent to his spirit, but a wise man quietly holds it back.*
(Proverbs 29:11 ESV)

#  11   Enjoy Your Family

Constant noise has become many people's companions. They tune into their devices so they can remain connected to everything outside of their world. As a result, however, they can become much more disconnected from everything inside their own world. That's why I want to remind you that you don't need to constantly know what is happening outside of your circle of influence. Turn off electronic devices occasionally, not so you can become insular, but so you can focus on what matters in life. As Louis Zamperini stated, "The world, we discovered, doesn't love you like your family loves you." The love of family is unconditional—so invest in those people first.

> How often do you allow your cell phone to draw you away from focusing on your family?

*I will not set before my eyes anything that is worthless. I hate the work of those who fall away; it shall not cling to me.* (Psalm 101:3 ESV)

# 12 Peace

In a book on stress, Doctor Richard Swenson made this statement: "No people in the history of humankind has ever had to live with the stressors we have acting upon us today. The human spirit is called upon to withstand pressures that have never before been encountered." There's no doubt about it. We're living in an age in which fear, anxiety, and pressure are moment by moment realities for most people. The good news is, it's possible to live each day with something the Bible calls "peace." It's a peace that the book of Philippians says defies our ability to explain or understand. You can live in the eye of the hurricane of life.

## Do you need the touch of God's peace in your life?

*Now the Lord of peace himself give you peace always by all means. The Lord be with you all.* (2 Thessalonians 3:16 KJV)

**13** Divorce Isn't an Option

Divorce is shockingly easy to obtain in our society today. Gone is any social stigma associated with it. But if you're going to beat the odds and make your marriage a lasting and fulfilling one, you must make a quality decision that divorce is not an option for you. The first attitude adjustment you must make on the road to a winning marriage is—forget about divorce. If you are trying to convince yourself that things will be easier with someone else, the odds are strongly against you.

Have you made the decision that divorce won't be an easy out when you run into difficulties in your marriage?

*He answered, "Have you not read that he who created them from the beginning made them male and female, and said, 'Therefore a man shall leave his father and his mother and hold fast to his wife, and the two shall become one flesh'? So they are no longer two but one flesh. What therefore God has joined together, let not man separate."* (Matthew 19:4–6 ESV)

## 14 Acceptance

Can you think of someone you'd like to influence in a positive way? If you're like most people, you have one or more individuals in your life you desperately want to impact in a positive way. If you're a parent, it's probably your children. Or perhaps it's a friend, coworker, or neighbor. No matter who you want to impact, one fact remains—no one is going to be open to your influence unless they feel unconditionally accepted. If your children feel your love is somehow tied to their performance, you'll never wield the level of influence in their lives that will help you keep them clear of life's pitfalls. Unconditional acceptance—it's a key to exercising positive influence.

Do you have conditions attached to your love or do you love people for who they really are?

*Greater love hath no man than this, that a man lay down his life for his friends.* (John 15:13 KJV)

# Never Stop Dreaming

C.S. Lewis once said, "You are never too old to set another goal or to dream a new dream." Whether you are thirty, fifty, or eighty—as long as you are on this earth, you can still pursue your dreams. One of the best examples I know of this truth is none other than my very own dad. At age 85, he decided to begin training as a short-distance runner. From 2001 to 2008, he successfully competed in the Georgia and Minnesota Senior Olympic Games. He won three silver medals and seven gold medals. Six of those medals came when he was 93! He would want me to remind you today that you are never too old to stop dreaming.

## What are you dreaming about and how can you put wings to those dreams?

*But as it is written, Eye hath not seen, nor ear heard, neither have entered into the heart of man, the things which God hath prepared for them that love him. But God hath revealed them unto us by his Spirit: for the Spirit searcheth all things, yea, the deep things of God.* (1 Corinthians 2:9–10 KJV)

Image • Rob Schrader

# 16 Be Loyal Despite Disagreement

It's easy to go along with leadership when you agree with the direction that's been set. The true test comes when you think you have a better idea. That's where the quality called loyalty comes in. When leaders look for those they can entrust with increased responsibility, one of the most important, yet rare, traits they look for is loyalty. The loyal person seeks to advance the best interests and goals of the leader. And true loyalty is never tested or made manifest until leadership sets a course with which you disagree. The Bible calls it submission to proper authority and giving honor to whom honor is due. It's also a rare quality that will get you promoted.

How do you respond when someone in authority has a different plan than you do?

*Honour all men. Love the brotherhood. Fear God. Honour the king.*
(1 Peter 2:17 KJV)

#  Unconditional Love

Do you need to be a more effective influence on those around you? You'll find your ability to lead others soaring when they know that you love them unconditionally. This is one of the leadership secrets of Jesus. Jesus experienced rejection, criticism, and even betrayal, but His acceptance of others was unwavering. When those you lead know your acceptance and care won't be withdrawn when they make a mistake or disagree, you'll find them responding to your leadership as never before.

## Do your people sense your unconditional acceptance?

*Hereby perceive we the love of God, because he laid down his life for us: and we ought to lay down our lives for the brethren.* (1 John 3:16 KJV)

# 18 Influence Begins With Words

Would you like to be a more influential person? Influence is something of which all of us could use more. Influence gives you the ability to guide your children away from pitfalls and destructive behavior patterns, gives you leverage on the job, and offers you opportunities to make your community a better place to live. If you want to wield more influence, you're going to have to become a better communicator. In the book of Proverbs, one of the wisest men who ever lived wrote, "Righteous lips are the delight of kings; and they love him that speaketh right." That means, the key to having positive influence with decision makers and people in authority lies a few short inches beneath your nose. Influence begins with the words you speak.

## How are the words you speak influencing others: for evil or for good?

*There are those who speak rashly, like the piercing of a sword, but the tongue of the wise brings healing.* (Proverbs 12:18 Amp.)

## 19 Try Church Again

Some people's experiences with church have prompted them to attend with regularity; other people's experiences have driven them away. If you're in the latter group, go ahead and try church again. A wide variety of churches are available nowadays. Some have contemporary music; others stick with traditional. Preachers wear everything from ripped skinny jeans and a suit coat to traditional priestly robes. If you keep looking, you will be able to find a church you and your family like... and I encourage you to do so, for church is your opportunity to connect with almighty God. He wants you to experience His love, peace, and joy in your life.

Have you believed the lie that church isn't worth your time?

*This is not the time to pull away and neglect meeting together, as some have formed the habit of doing, because we need each other! In fact, we should come together even more frequently, eager to encourage and urge each other onward as we anticipate that day dawning.* (Hebrews 10:25 TPT)

# Time Doesn't Constrain God

Some assume if they can't see an answer to their prayers, God must have answered their prayers with a "no." However, prayers aren't always realized within the time period we expect. That's why I recommend you heed these words from Nathan Grams: "Don't retire a prayer until God is done with it." Keep bringing uncertainty and concern to the Lord, and then trust that He will answer the prayer in the way that is best for all involved. His timing may look different, for God doesn't have a limited life as we do. He understands how to answer your prayers with eternity in mind. That's why Tara Leigh Cobble stated, "God is not constrained by time. He invented it."

## Has an unanswered prayer stopped you from trusting in God?

*For my thoughts are not your thoughts, neither are your ways my ways, saith the Lord. For as the heavens are higher than the earth, so are my ways higher than your ways, and my thoughts than your thoughts.* (Isaiah 55:8–9 KJV)

# 21 The Prevailing Factor of Success

It's easy to think that the smartest, brightest, and most talented will be the most successful, but that's not necessarily the case. Just as in the case of the tortoise and the hare, the person who wins is the person who never gives up. President Calvin Coolidge pointed out this fact when he said, "Nothing in this world can take the place of persistence. Talent will not; nothing is more common than unsuccessful people with talent. Genius will not; unrewarded genius is almost a proverb. Education will not; the world is full of educated failures. Persistence and determination alone are omnipotent." President Coolidge was absolutely right.

What prevails in your life: talent or determination?

*For the righteous falls seven times and rises again, but the wicked stumble in times of calamity.* (Proverbs 24:16 ESV)

#  Use Your Time Wisely

Did you know that you can identify people's interests by watching how they spend their time? People who love to shop make it a priority to head to the mall, and golfers can always be found on the golf course. Their love for their hobbies comes through in the way they invest their time. The same is true for you. Where you invest your time shows what you think is important. If you say your family is important, but never spend time with them, then your actions speak louder than your words. Your schedule shows others your priorities. Motivational speaker Harvey Mackay put it this way: "Decide what your priorities are and how much time you'll spend on them. If you don't, someone else will."

## Where are you investing your life?

*So teach us to number our days, that we may get us a heart of wisdom.*
(Psalm 90:12 Amp.)

## ㉓ Don't Keep an Offense

Has anything irritated you lately? Perhaps something has annoyed or angered you. If so, according to the dictionary, you've come face to face with the opportunity to take offense. Offense is deadly. It comes in a blaze of emotions, blinds you to the truth of a situation, and mires you in frustration—all because you don't like what someone else said or did. The reality, though, is that everyone has a different opinion. We have to get used to the multiple opportunities to dislike each other's actions and simply choose to live above offense. As Abraham Lincoln stated, "We should be too big to take offense and too noble to give it."

Are you doing everything you can to keep offenses far from you?

*The discretion of a man deferreth his anger; and it is his glory to pass over a transgression.* (Proverbs 19:11 KJV)

#  Discontentment Isn't Worth It

Discontentment has become a commodity nowadays. The more discontent you can be, the more attention you can receive. Rewarding discontent, however, simultaneously rewards attitudes of entitlement and victimhood—and these two mindsets are dangerous, for they place control of your life in the hands of others. Any time your life is solely in other people's control, frustration follows. That's why I recommend the path of contentment instead. Contentment places a priority on personal responsibility. It knows that others won't always treat you well—and you won't always get what you deserve—but you can always be grateful for what you have.

## How can you show the people around you that you believe in them today?

*Keep your life free from love of money, and be content with what you have, for he has said, "I will never leave you nor forsake you."* (Hebrews 13:5 ESV)

# It Takes Courage to Have Character

"Courage is not simply one of the virtues, but the form of every virtue at the testing point." C.S. Lewis' observation is interesting; it takes courage to be a person of character. Taking this "high road" isn't easy, but being a person of quality character will set you on the pathway to success. It's one thing, though, to say you are a person of character; it's another thing to live it. Consider what Thomas Jefferson said: "Action will delineate and define you." If you want to be a person of character, put action to your intent. It will set you apart from a crowd.

## Are you courageous enough to be a person of strong character?

*...Make every effort to supplement your faith with virtue, and virtue with knowledge, and knowledge with self-control, and self-control with steadfastness, and steadfastness with godliness, and godliness with brotherly affection, and brotherly affection with love.* (2 Peter 1:5–7 ESV)

#  26 Avoid Hypocrisy

Benjamin Franklin once said, "It is easier to exemplify values than to teach them." That's especially true where our children are concerned. Many parents tell their children what to do and even correct them when they do wrong. But many fail at the most important aspect of training—modeling the value system they are trying to teach their children. It's hypocritical to tell your children one thing and do another. If you demand honesty and then cheat on your taxes, your actions undermine your words. But when your life demonstrates the ideals you espouse, you're doubly influential.

## Are you modeling the values you teach?

*How can you think of saying to your friend, "Let me help you get rid of that speck in your eye," when you can't see past the log in your own eye? Hypocrite! First get rid of the log in your own eye; then you will see well enough to deal with the speck in your friend's eye. (Matthew 7:4–5 NLT)*

## 27 Purpose

Few people achieve the level of success of which they are capable. Why? Because they lack the vital ingredient of purpose. In 1872, the great British Prime Minister Benjamin Disraeli made this statement: "The secret of success is constancy of purpose." He may not have known it, but when he made that statement, he was speaking a biblical truth. In Philippians 2:2, we are commanded to be "united in spirit, intent on one purpose." Throughout the Bible, we see that the men and women who achieve great things do so by making God's purpose their purpose. Discover God's purpose for your life then pursue it single-mindedly. It will make you a winner in every area of life.

### Have you discovered God's purpose for your life?

*For I know the thoughts that I think toward you, saith the Lord, thoughts of peace, and not of evil, to give you an expected end.* (Jeremiah 29:11 KJV)

#  28   Speak With Discretion

How would you like a foolproof method for avoiding trouble? Listen to this advice. An old Spanish proverb says, "The fish dies because he opens his mouth." Proverbs 21:23 reads, "He who guards his mouth and his tongue, guards his soul from troubles." How many times has your mouth gotten you in trouble? If you're like most people, you've done this more times than you can count. But according to the Word of God, you can learn to guard what you say and by doing so, you can stay out of trouble and avoid a lot of unnecessary pain and grief.

> Are you being wise with the words that you speak?

*Watch your tongue and keep your mouth shut, and you will stay out of trouble.* (Proverbs 21:23 NLT)

**Knowing Others**

I have an important question for you, one with implications for your happiness and quality of life. The question is: How many people do you know? Before you answer, realize I didn't ask, "How many people are you acquainted with?" I asked, how many people do you "know"? Healthy relationships are the channels through which God brings nearly all of the good things of life. A fundamental key to building strong relationships is really "knowing" people. The Bible in 2 Corinthians 5:16 instructs us to "know no man after the flesh." What God is telling us there is that you don't really know someone if all you know is the outward facade.

Do you take the time to get to know people beyond their outward facades?

*So we have stopped evaluating others from a human point of view. At one time we thought of Christ merely from a human point of view. How differently we know him now!* (2 Corinthians 5:16 NLT)

#  30 Avoid Sluggishness

Life isn't boring. Work isn't meaningless. Relationships aren't valueless. All of these statements are true for the person who knows the key to self-motivation. Bored, unenthusiastic, unmotivated people wear depressing qualities on their shirtsleeves for the whole world to see—and catch. They are always looking for better jobs, more exciting relationships, or an environment that appreciates them. It rarely works that way. These people usually infect everything and everyone around them with the disease of sluggishness. Not surprisingly, such people are the last in line for promotion and leadership opportunities. To be a standout on the job, be contagiously motivated.

Have you allowed sluggishness to affect your everyday life?

*The soul of the sluggard craves and gets nothing, while the soul of the diligent is richly supplied.* (Proverbs 13:4 ESV)

# 31 Act

Being a person of action is a common attribute of those who grow in responsibility and reward. Charles Dickens once said, "Whatever I have tried to do in my life, I have tried with all my heart to do it well. Whatever I have devoted myself to, I have devoted myself completely." Here Dickens has articulated a success formula that will work for any individual in any setting. A person of action such as this will make things happen. They'll see opportunities others overlook and seize them. They'll be what the book of Proverbs repeatedly describes as "bold and diligent...." It's the kind of person who tends to shine as a star at work.

## Are you diligent in your efforts at work?

*Work hard so you can present yourself to God and receive his approval. Be a good worker, one who does not need to be ashamed and who correctly explains the word of truth.* (2 Timothy 2:15 NLT)

AUGUST

Image • Brandon Cormier

# 1  Be Tenacious

One skill outstanding leaders possess is persistence—the tenacity to keep driving toward goals. People who risk making changes and pursue lofty goals not only succeed more often, they also fail more often. But effective leaders are so completely committed to their vision that they see setbacks as opportunities rather than dead ends. When they fall down, they pick themselves up, figure out why they fell, and try again. That's why the book of Romans encourages us to pray for perseverance and seek encouragement from God.

Have you asked God to help you develop a leader's tenacity?

*And let us not be weary in well doing: for in due season we shall reap, if we faint not.* (Galatians 6:9 KJV)

# 2   What's Your Instinct?

Some of the best examples of winning in life come right in the middle of tragedy. Take, for example, the 14-year-old boy who rescued his neighbor's eight-year-old son from his burning home. Or the father and son who lost everything in Hurricane Isaac, but chose not to focus on that. Instead, they risked their lives by using a friend's boat to help 120 people stranded by floodwaters. These people didn't have time to ponder what decision was right when adversity came. They instinctively made the decision to put others in front of their own selves. I encourage you to follow these examples. Start living your life now by putting others in front of yourself so your natural instinct—in daily life and in difficulty—will be to turn your eyes outward.

> ## Who is first in your thinking: others or yourself?

*Beloved, let us love one another, for love is from God, and whoever loves has been born of God and knows God. Anyone who does not love does not know God, because God is love.* (1 John 4:7–8 ESV)

# ③ Look for Potential Leaders

The best predictor of the future is the past. That's why when it comes time to look for people in your organization who are ready to be elevated to leadership, one of the key traits to look for is a history of leadership, even in small things. One wise business owner told me he took note of any worker who said he was a deacon in his church or a **Boy Scout** leader. If he showed leadership outside of the job, he would probably exhibit it on the job. The Bible says, "The person who is faithful in a little thing will be faithful in big things, too."

Are you seeing potential leaders in those with a history of leading in little things?

*He that is faithful in that which is least is faithful also in much: and he that is unjust in the least is unjust also in much.* (Luke 16:10 KJV)

#  Stay in the Press

The winning life isn't a casual stroll; it's a press. The need to press is deeply rooted in the reality of our daily lives. There's a press to make relationships work and a press to keep your body healthy and functioning properly. There's a press to succeed in your vocation or business. In the Bible, the apostle Paul talks about another kind of press. He says, "I press toward the mark for the prize of the high calling of God in Christ Jesus." Here Paul lays out a guideline to help us succeed in every area of human endeavor. If you're successful in this press, everything else in life falls into place.

## Are you prepared to press?

*For you have need of endurance, so that when you have done the will of God you may receive what is promised.* (Hebrews 10:36 ESV)

# 5 Put Aside the Past

One of the quickest ways to slow your momentum in life is to get stuck in your past. Decisions you regret or mistakes you make can create a pervading sense of unworthiness and a negative expectation for your future. The truth, however, is different: Your past does not need to control your future. You can deliberately choose to put the past out of mind. Choose not to think about that which could bring you down or slow your momentum. As the apostle Paul wrote in Philippians chapter 3, "...this one thing I do, forgetting those things which are behind, and reaching forth unto those things which are before, I press toward the mark for the prize of the high calling of God in Christ Jesus."

## Are you living in your past or looking forward to your future?

*I don't mean to say that I have already achieved these things or that I have already reached perfection. But I press on to possess that perfection for which Christ Jesus first possessed me.* (Philippians 3:12 NLT)

# 6   Value Others

If someone handed you a $100 bill, what would you do with it? Most likely, you would smile, say "Thank you," and put it in your wallet because you recognize the inherent value of that piece of paper. I want to challenge you today to consider looking at your leaders with a similar valuation to what you have for that $100 bill. Value the fact that they are willing to be held to a higher standard, be put under greater scrutiny, lead through difficulties, and bring desired results. Even if the leaders in your life don't appear to deserve your respect, respect the office in which they are in—and remember what John Maxwell said: "You add value to people when you value them."

## How do you view those around you?

*Iron sharpeneth iron; so a man sharpeneth the countenance of his friend.*
(Proverbs 27:17 KJV)

# Leave the Past Behind

The quickest way to get into discouragement and despair is to focus on past disappointments—so don't do it! Don't dwell on the disappointment you felt when you didn't get that promotion. Don't keep mentally rehearsing those words of rejection that were spoken to you. Those memories will put you on the fast track to despair, deception, or worse. Even thoughts about the good things in the past can trip you up. They can lead you to disappointment about your current situation if it's not quite as bright as in days gone by. Good or bad, you must leave the past behind—for your focus determines your destiny.

## What are you focused on today?

*Therefore if any man be in Christ, he is a new creature: old things are passed away; behold, all things are become new.* (2 Corinthians 5:17 KJV)

#  Take the Path Less Walked

When advising a woman who was dealing with patent infringements in her business, Mark Cuban suggested, "Don't go after the businesses. Out compete. How you respond to roadblocks is exactly what guides your future." Washington Irving also understood the importance of dealing correctly with adversity. He stated, "Little minds are tamed and subdued by misfortune, but great minds rise above them." Even the book of Proverbs agrees: it says "It is an honor for a man to cease from strife and keep aloof from it, but every fool will quarrel." How you respond to adversity will absolutely affect the rest of your life. If you want to walk the path of success, be honorable and rise above difficulty.

## What path do you take when you face adversity?

*Anyone who meets a testing challenge head-on and manages to stick it out is mighty fortunate. For such persons loyally in love with God, the reward is life and more life.* (James 1:12 Msg.)

# ⑨  Don't Compare

Scrolling through social media feeds can be interesting as you catch up on other people's lives. It can also be frustrating if you find yourself comparing the highlights of other people's lives to everything you are facing right now. Steven Furtick put it this way: "The reason we struggle with insecurity is because we compare our behind-the-scenes with everyone else's highlight reel." Theodore Roosevelt once said, "Comparison is the thief of joy." He's absolutely right. If you want to become sad and frustrated, compare your life to those around you and never think about the possibility that they are dealing with something difficult you can't see. So I encourage you, live your life free from comparison.

## Have you let comparison dictate how you feel?

*For we dare not make ourselves of the number, or compare ourselves with some that commend themselves: but they measuring themselves by themselves, and comparing themselves among themselves, are not wise.* (2 Corinthians 10:12 KJV)

# Relationships Enhance Our Lives

Redwood trees are the tallest in the world. Since each tree can grow to over 300 feet, one may assume that each tree's root system goes down comparatively deep—but that would be an incorrect assumption. The roots of a Redwood tree only go down about ten feet underground. The ability to grow over 300 feet comes from the fact that each tree's roots are interconnected with other trees nearby. This networking of roots provides the stability for the trees to ascend as high as they do. What a great example of the truth that a life that is integrated well with other people will be able to ascend to great heights. You could also say, relationships with quality people enable us to grow.

## How far do your roots of relationships extend?

*In this way we are like the various parts of a human body. Each part gets its meaning from the body as a whole, not the other way around. The body we're talking about is Christ's body of chosen people. Each of us finds our meaning and function as a part of his body. But as a chopped-off finger or cut-off toe we wouldn't amount to much, would we? So since we find ourselves fashioned into all these excellently formed and marvelously functioning parts in Christ's body, let's just go ahead and be what we were made to be, without enviously or pridefully comparing ourselves with each other, or trying to be something we aren't.*

(Romans 12:4–6 Msg.)

# Where a Successful Job Begins

An idea is floating around that you'll be at your best when you find your ideal job. I want you to consider that from a different perspective today: your ideal job won't be found until you give your current job your best. Your attitude, competency, and effort all create the experience that you receive from your 9–5 job. If you're not functioning with the exact job description you'd like right now, that doesn't give you the excuse to give less. In fact, it should propel you to do more. Maya Angelou put it this way: "If you don't like something, change it. If you can't change it, change your attitude." So always remember: success in the workplace starts with you.

Do you need to make a change
in the way you view your work?

*Now you're dressed in a new wardrobe. Every item of your new way of life is custom-made by the Creator, with his label on it.* (Colossians 3:10 Msg.)

# 12 Think of Others First

There's a thin line between confidence and arrogance. It's called humility. You could describe the difference like this: Confidence smiles. Arrogance smirks. Humble people exude confidence because they stand by their values. They can listen to other people's advice and bend their methods for reaching their goals, but they also know their boundaries. They understand they do not need to become a floor mat anyone can walk on. C.S. Lewis stated, "Humility is not thinking less of yourself; it's thinking of yourself less."

## Do people consider you to be humble?

*And Jesus called them to him and said to them, "You know that those who are considered rulers of the Gentiles lord it over them, and their great ones exercise authority over them. But it shall not be so among you. But whoever would be great among you must be your servant, and whoever would be first among you must be slave of all. For even the Son of Man came not to be served but to serve, and to give his life as a ransom for many." (Mark 10:42–45 ESV)*

# 13 Don't Be a "Phubber"

Have you ever been "phubbed"? It's a word someone coined in 2012 to combine the words "phone" and "snubbed." It refers to when you're sitting next to someone who is paying more attention to a phone than to you. "Phubbing"—or let's just call it "phone snubbing"—shows that whoever is on the other side of that text, phone call, or even Internet page is more interesting than the person you are with physically. Focusing on electronics over people is both rude and selfish. It's time we start choosing to pay attention to the people we are with physically, not the people we can talk to virtually. If you want to win in life, be physically—and mentally—present when you are with people.

> Have you ever been guilty of ignoring someone in favor of your phone?

*Love is patient and kind; love does not envy or boast; it is not arrogant or rude. It does not insist on its own way; it is not irritable or resentful.*

(1 Corinthians 13:4–5 ESV)

# 14 Submission=Success, Part 1

When speaking at Arlington National Cemetery on Memorial Day in 1924, President Calvin Coolidge said, "When each citizen submits himself to the authority of law, he does not thereby decrease his independence or freedom, but rather increases it. [When he recognizes] that he is a part of a larger body which is banded together for a common purpose, he becomes more than an individual; he rises to a new dignity of citizenship." You and I are just one part of a nation filled with people who have come together to form one country—a country that operates better with public laws and authority put in place to enforce those laws. Let's always remember and respect that truth.

## What's your view of submission?

*Be a good citizen. All governments are under God. Insofar as there is peace and order, it's God's order. So live responsibly as a citizen.* (Romans 13:1 Msg.)

#  Submission=Success, Part 2

During his speech in 1924, President Calvin Coolidge talked about what happens when a citizen submits himself to the authority of law. "Instead of finding himself restricted and confined by rendering obedience to public law, he finds himself protected and defended and in the exercise of increased and increasing rights." Submission to authority isn't blind obedience; it's also not acceptance of abuse. Submission is an attitude of the heart that recognizes the need for authority in our lives. You may not always agree with your leaders, but it is in your best interest to submit yourself to them. Submission sets you up for success.

### Are you submitted to the authority figures in your life?

*Remind the believers to submit to the government and its officers. They should be obedient, always ready to do what is good. They must not slander anyone and must avoid quarreling. Instead, they should be gentle and show true humility to everyone. (Titus 3:1–2 NLT)*

# 16 The Power of Patience

The pace of today's society often appears more appealing than the road of patience—but you'll never experience growth if you don't learn to wait. Although you may be physically inactive while waiting for change, the process of patience is actually not inactive. Patience releases a power for change that cannot be duplicated. The best example of this is agriculture. When a farmer places a seed in the ground, patience empowers that seed to grow. Impatience would only stunt growth and limit his harvest. Benjamin Franklin understood this power; he stated, "He that can have patience can have what he will."

## Have you unlocked the potential of patience?

*And we desire that every one of you do shew the same diligence to the full assurance of hope unto the end: that ye be not slothful, but followers of them who through faith and patience inherit the promises.* (Hebrews 6:11–12 KJV)

#  Put Unity First

Henry Ford once said, "Coming together is a beginning. Keeping together is progress. Working together is success." He's absolutely right, the key element that will make working together a possibility—unity. Unity must be in place if you want to create a productive work environment. This doesn't mean we all need to think the same thoughts and never disagree. As Martin Luther King Jr. said, "Unity has never meant uniformity." What unity does mean is that we come together with our unique opinions to support a common cause. My encouragement for you today is that whether you are a leader or an employee, promoting unity will always be in your best interests.

What can you do to maintain unity in your relationships?

*Behold, how good and how pleasant it is for brethren to dwell together in unity!*
(Psalm 133:1 KJV)

## 18 Today Can Be a Better Day

It's easy to get caught up in the past, particularly if your future seems blocked by an insurmountable wall of financial difficulty, societal inequality, or some other circumstance that has left you feeling hopeless. The good news is, no matter how hard you fall or how far you've fallen, you can get back up again. Writer Oscar Wilde once said, "What seems to us as bitter trials are often blessings in disguise." Although your circumstance may not disappear overnight, a negative attitude can. Look at the difficulty you see as an opportunity in disguise. As the saying goes, your best days are truly ahead of you.

### Are you ready to let today be a good day?

*Remember not the former things, nor consider the things of old. Behold, I am doing a new thing; now it springs forth, do you not perceive it? I will make a way in the wilderness and rivers in the desert.* (Isaiah 43:18–19 ESV)

# 19 Be Gentle

Over time, people have come to associate the word gentle with weak or soft, but the dictionary's definition includes the original meaning of gentleness—honorable, distinguished, kind, and chivalrous. One of the greatest characteristics that could be ascribed to both men and women is the characteristic of gentleness. When you are gentle, your strength is under control. You don't intimidate; you inspire. You don't instill fear, but faith. Saint Francis de Sales put it this way: "Nothing is so strong as gentleness. Nothing so gentle as real strength."

## Do people consider you gentle?

*But the fruit of the Spirit is love, joy, peace, longsuffering, gentleness, goodness, faith, meekness, temperance: against such there is no law.*
(Galatians 5:22–23 KJV)

# How Do You Fit Into the Team?

Who is the most important player on a team—the basketball superstar who made the three-point shot or the guard who set up the screen that made the shot possible? The superstars of a team are often the ones who get a lot of attention, but their winning stats would not be possible unless they were surrounded by players who made it possible to score. In the same way, your job is a team effort between you, your coworkers, and your leaders. We all have a contribution to make. As Helen Keller once said, "Alone we can do so little; together we can do so much." Your team will work best when you understand your position and fulfill it to the best of your ability.

Have you taken the time to determine how you best fit into your workplace?

*If the foot shall say, Because I am not the hand, I am not of the body; is it therefore not of the body? And if the ear shall say, Because I am not the eye, I am not of the body; is it therefore not of the body? If the whole body were an eye, where were the hearing? If the whole were hearing, where were the smelling? But now hath God set the members every one of them in the body, as it hath pleased him. And if they were all one member, where were the body? But now are they many members, yet but one body.*

(1 Corinthians 12:15–20 KJV)

#  Interest vs. Commitment

There is a difference between mere interest and commitment. When you're interested in doing something, you do it only when it's convenient. When you're committed to something, you accept no excuses, only results. Commitment is an attribute wise leaders look for in those they elevate to positions of leadership. Commitment has an almost supernatural ability to make things happen for you. As Napoleon Hill once said, "The moment you commit and quit holding back, all sorts of unforeseen incidents, meetings, and material assistance will rise up to help you. The simple act of commitment is a powerful magnet for help."

## Does your commitment extend beyond convenience?

*So let's keep focused on that goal, those of us who want everything God has for us. If any of you have something else in mind, something less than total commitment, God will clear your blurred vision—you'll see it yet! Now that we're on the right track, let's stay on it.* (Philippians 3:15–16 Msg.)

## 22 Get Creative

In 1990, Southwest Airlines adopted a new slogan: "Just Plane Smart." What they didn't realize is the phrase "Plane Smart" was already being used by Stevens Aviation. When chairman Kurt Herwald found this out, he recognized neither company would benefit from a legal battle. So, instead, he challenged the CEO of Southwest to an arm-wrestling match for the rights to the slogan. The loser would donate $5,000 to charity. In the end, the heavily-promoted match ended up increasing the profitability—and likability—for both companies. It's a good reminder that conflict can be creatively resolved when you think outside the box.

Is there a relationship or problem in your life that you can solve by taking time to think about it creatively?

*Through wisdom is an house builded; and by understanding it is established: and by knowledge shall the chambers be filled with all precious and pleasant riches.*
(Proverbs 24:3–4 KJV)

#  Actively Value Good Relationships

Any time you deal with people, things can get difficult. Arguments and discussions, expectations and disappointments—all of these things can tempt us to shy away from people. The reality, though, is that we need each other. We need each other's input. We can learn from each other's experiences. Without others, we would have no one to laugh with, no one to cry with, no one to celebrate with. The people in our lives make the journey in life more enjoyable and even possible. As Theodore Roosevelt said, "The most important single ingredient in the formula of success is knowing how to get along with people." Misunderstandings and conflict will come and go, but we should never underestimate the value of good relationships.

## What is one thing you can do that shows others in your life that you value them?

*You're blessed when you can show people how to cooperate instead of compete or fight. That's when you discover who you really are, and your place in God's family.* (Matthew 5:9 Msg.)

The Power of a Pause

Did you know that a great stress reliever is simply giving yourself time to think? You can better handle the stress of life when you purposefully "pause" and identify where your time is going as well as where you'd actually like it to go. A pause gives you both the time and ability to act and not simply react. For some of you, that pause may be ten or fifteen minutes taken early in the morning right after you wake up. For others, it may be best when you head into the office. Some of you may take a few minutes multiple times a day. Find out what works for you and plan your day accordingly. Living with a "pause" in place will help you weed out excess noise and hone in your daily activity to what truly matters.

Have you put the power of a pause into your life?

*Come to me, all who labor and are heavy laden, and I will give you rest.* (Matthew 11:28 ESV)

#  Redefining the "End of the Road"

In the mid-20th century, people stopped using coal to heat their homes. The switch to oil and gas furnaces helped their walls stay clean from soot, and as a result, they no longer needed wallpaper cleaner. That meant Cleo McVicker's successful wallpaper cleaner company was headed for a dead end. Things changed in 1954 when a family member discovered that a few tweaks turned this doughy-substance of wallpaper cleaner into a great children's toy. She recommended the business change directions and even supplied a new name: Play-Doh. What a great reminder to always look around the corner to see what may be coming next. What seems like the end of the road may only be a sharp curve in a different direction or a new beginning.

Is there a place in your life that needs to be redefined from the "end" to the "beginning"?

*One day Jesus told his disciples a story to show that they should always pray and never give up. "There was a judge in a certain city," he said, "who neither feared God nor cared about people. A widow of that city came to him repeatedly, saying, 'Give me justice in this dispute with my enemy.' The judge ignored her for a while, but finally he said to himself, 'I don't fear God or care about people, but this woman is driving me crazy. I'm going to see that she gets justice, because she is wearing me out with her constant requests!'"*

(Luke 18:1–5 NLT)

#  26   Choose Forgiveness Daily

An emotional wound needs time to heal—but that wound will not heal if you continually rip it open through remembering how horrible the other person treated you. A man by the name of David Ridge put it this way: "True forgiveness is not an action after the fact; it is an attitude with which you enter each moment." With every day that passes, you will have the opportunity to think negative thoughts about people you've forgiven in the past. Instead of allowing those thoughts to replay in your head, make a point to think positively. As you deliberately choose forgiveness on a daily basis, you'll enable yourself to heal and the relationship to grow.

## Have you given yourself the time you need to heal well?

*Then came Peter to him, and said, Lord, how oft shall my brother sin against me, and I forgive him? till seven times? Jesus saith unto him, I say not unto thee, Until seven times: but, Until seventy times seven.* (Matthew 18:21–22 KJV)

# The Power of a Compliment

Do you want an easy way to strengthen a relationship? Give someone a compliment. Compliments encourage everyone and can greatly impact someone's mood. In fact, Mark Twain once said, "I can live two months on a good compliment." Write a note, give someone a call, or send an email to let people know when they are doing a good job. Compliments are free and easy to give. All it takes is the courage to speak up. Plus, consider what Henry David Thoreau stated: "The greatest compliment that was ever paid me was when one asked what I thought and attended to my answer."

Will you take advantage of your opportunity to impact someone's life by embracing the power of a compliment?

*Worry weighs a person down; an encouraging word cheers a person up.*
(Proverbs 12:25 NLT)

# What Comes First?

When Neil Blumenthal cofounded the online glasses company Warby Parker with two of his friends, the three of them made a pact to stay friends through the business process. They knew too many stories of friends who went into business together then ended up at each other's throats or in court. They met monthly in the same place to provide feedback, air grievances, and give recommendations. Their proactive approach to put people before business helped them to treat each other respectfully and address situations before they became a big deal. It's another lesson we can learn as we strive to win in our relationships.

## Have you taken steps to protect your priorities in life?

*God is love. When we take up permanent residence in a life of love, we live in God and God lives in us. This way, love has the run of the house, becomes at home and mature in us, so that we're free of worry on Judgment Day—our standing in the world is identical with Christ's.* (1 John 4:16–17 Msg)

#  Integrity Will Be Rewarded

In Proverbs 11:3, King Solomon, writing by inspiration of God says, "The integrity of the upright guides them, but the unfaithful are destroyed by their duplicity." Webster defines integrity as "strict personal honesty." And according to the verse we just heard, if you'll cultivate the quality of integrity, it will guide you through the most difficult of times and decisions. It takes courage to walk in integrity, but as Solomon reminds us, the rewards are great.

## Have you experienced the rewards integrity brings?

*People with integrity walk safely, but those who follow crooked paths will slip and fall.* (Proverbs 10:9 NLT)

# Where Change Starts

Successful people don't let every thought run through their heads without rein. They take the time to tame their brains—and you can do the same. If you're angry at someone, avoid focusing your thoughts on your anger. Instead, think about how you can creatively restore the relationship. If you're a recovering addict, don't allow yourself to think about how good another drink would be. Choose to think about your family, your health, and other goals you have created for yourself to strengthen your resolve to stay away. Whatever you are facing, purposefully redirect your thoughts to what is beneficial to you. As Norman Vincent Peale said, "Change your thoughts and you change your world."

Are you willing to change your life by changing your thinking?

*Casting down imaginations, and every high thing that exalteth itself against the knowledge of God, and bringing into captivity every thought to the obedience of Christ.* (2 Corinthians 10:5 KJV)

# 31 Imagine That!

Would you like to have the ability to perceive new business opportunities? Would you like to be able to find solutions to difficult problems no one else has even considered? Then what you need is imagination. The great leaders of the Bible all had the ability to look beyond present circumstances and see the possible. In other words, they had imagination. Many others have recognized its power. Einstein once said, "To see new possibilities, to regard old problems from a new angle, requires creative imagination."

## What are you doing to cultivate your God-given gift of imagination?

*And the Lord said, Behold, the people is one, and they have all one language; and this they begin to do: and now nothing will be restrained from them, which they have imagined to do.* (Genesis 11:6 KJV)

SEPTEMBER

Image • Baltimore Medina

# 1 Network

"It's not what you know; it's who you know." Never has this statement proven more true than in the career path of actor Harrison Ford. His career started with small roles in films. He became dissatisfied with the roles he was getting, so he chose a different path. He became a carpenter so he could support his family. Little did he know that his big break would eventually come from a carpentry job: he was hired to build cabinets at the home of George Lucas. As you may know, Lucas was the one who cast Ford in *Star Wars*, which launched Ford into the leading actor position. It's an excellent reminder that your relationships help mold the path your life will take.

## Have you embraced the possibilities available through networking?

*And they devoted themselves to the apostles' teaching and the fellowship, to the breaking of bread and the prayers.* (Acts 2:42 ESV)

# 2 Do You Listen Well?

When someone disagrees with you, which part of you is more likely to spring into action—your mouth or your ears? James 1:19 in the Bible says, "...be swift to hear, slow to speak, and slow to wrath...." Most of the quarreling married couples I've counseled over the years did just the opposite. They were slow to hear, swift to speak, and extremely swift to get angry. When most people hear the word "communication," they think of talking, rather than listening; yet listening is the most powerful weapon in the winning communicator's arsenal. Listening says, "I value your viewpoint enough to hear what you have to say." When others know you care enough to listen, the defenses come down and winning communication can begin.

> Do you care enough about your family and friends to truly listen to what they have to say?

*Even a fool, when he holdeth his peace, is counted wise: and he that shutteth his lips is esteemed a man of understanding.* (Proverbs 17:28 KJV)

## 3 Don't Cheat

A man by the name of George Hammond once said, "Resorting to lying or cheating in any competition amounts to conceding defeat." It's a truth we all know, but sometimes want to pretend we didn't—cheaters never win. Cheating and deception often appear to be the easy route to money and success. The thought, *No one will ever know*, seems to ring through many people's ears—but it's not a reality. The truth—and the cheaters—will eventually be exposed. So when you see someone winning through doing it the wrong way, know that they will be found out. It's always in your best interest to walk the path of integrity.

> When you see a cheater win, do you panic or trust God through it?

*Don't wear yourself out trying to get rich; restrain yourself! Riches disappear in the blink of an eye; wealth sprouts wings and flies off into the wild blue yonder.* (Proverbs 23:4–5 Msg.)

#  4  Faith Is an Option

When circumstances go south or a doctor's report is less than ideal, the ensuing battle with fear can be overwhelming. That fear lures you to believe that the only option for your future is the one you don't want. That's why I want to remind you that fear is not the only option. You can choose to have faith. When you choose faith, you choose to believe what you cannot yet see. You choose to believe that good can happen, even if you don't know how, for as Elisabeth Elliot stated, "Faith does not eliminate questions, but faith knows where to take them." Faith understands that God can take any situation you face and turn it around for good.

### Where have you allowed fear to stay in your life?

*Now faith is the substance of things hoped for, the evidence of things not seen. For by it the elders obtained a good report. Through faith we understand that the worlds were framed by the word of God, so that things which are seen were not made of things which do appear.* (Hebrews 11:1–3 KJV)

# 5  Be a Problem Solver

How many people have you bumped into who are great at finding fault with everything that's going on? It's a frustrating characteristic, particularly within the workplace. Albert Einstein once said, "We cannot solve our problems with the same thinking we used when we created them." Good employees find ways to creatively solve problems. Even if they don't know the best answer right away, they will tackle a difficult project until the best answer shows up. They instinctively know that when you avoid problems, you avoid solutions. So if you want to become indispensable to your employer, don't find problems. Solve them.

How do you view problems: something you find or something you solve?

*And call upon me in the day of trouble; I will deliver you, and you shall glorify me.* (Psalm 50:15 ESV)

# 6 What's Your Mission?

The term "mission statement" is a familiar part of the modern vocabulary. Yet 2,000 years ago, Jesus modeled a key to successful leadership—and living—that goes to the heart of this issue. Jesus knew His mission and He never deviated from it. During a test in the wilderness, Jesus was presented with three attractive opportunities that would have diverted Him from His cause. They were opportunities that seemed to promise a shortcut to gratification. He wisely refused them. We must do the same.

> Do you have a clearly articulated mission, and are you willing to say "no" to appealing distractions on the way to fulfilling it?

*For the Son of man is come to seek and to save that which was lost.*
(Luke 19:10 KJV)

# 7  Respect Authority

Abraham Lincoln once said, "Nearly all men can stand adversity, but if you want to test a man's character, give him power." Because of the nature of authority, you will come across leaders who abuse and misuse their authority—but that is not an excuse to disrespect leaders in return. From the President to your employer to parents and police officers, we are surrounded by authority figures. You may not agree with each one of them, but agreement is not a prerequisite for respect. If you want to walk the pathway to success, look past your leaders' beliefs or political platform and respect the positions of authority in which they stand.

> Have you allowed your leaders' actions to alter your respect for them?

*Give to everyone what you owe them: Pay your taxes and government fees to those who collect them, and give respect and honor to those who are in authority.* (Romans 13:7 NLT)

#  8   Silence the Critics

Every fall, much of America gathers in front of the TV across the nation to cheer on their favorite football teams. We yell at the refs, root for our favorite players, and moan when the coaches call a play we don't like. It's as though we all become experts at the game that only has a few professionals. It's a good reminder for our daily lives that even when we are at the top of our game, critics will come out from all corners. Professional quarterback Peyton Manning knows that firsthand. His solution is, "If you work hard and you play well, all those critics quiet themselves pretty quickly." Let your work ethic outshine any criticism that will come your way.

## Do you let other people's opinions affect your work?

*For the Lord God will help me; therefore shall I not be confounded: therefore have I set my face like a flint, and I know that I shall not be ashamed.* (Isaiah 50:7 KJV)

# 9   Let Your Work Speak for Itself

It can be tempting to draw attention to our achievements in hopes we will get promoted or recognized in some way. The reality, though, is that when you work hard and dedicate yourself to accomplish your job, you won't need to hunt down promotion or rewards. They will come after you. Football great Walter Payton put it this way: "When you're good at something, you'll tell everyone. When you're great at something, they'll tell you." Let your talent and your hard work speak for itself. People will see what you bring to the table and call on you for help when they see a need for your gift. As the author of the book of Proverbs wrote, "A man's gift makes room for him, and brings him before great men."

Who promotes you the most: you or others?

*But God is the judge: he putteth down one, and setteth up another.*
(Psalm 75:7 KJV)

#  Stop the Excuses

If it's important to you, you will find a way. If not, you'll find an excuse. All people have an excuse as to why they can't do something, but not all have a reason as to why they can do it. Courage. Strength. Discipline. These are all reasons why you can accomplish what is in front of you—but they will only become a part of your life if you step past your excuses. As Teddy Bridgewater once posted on Twitter, "Be stronger than your strongest excuse." Whether it's meeting personal goals or progressing in your business, be determined.

## What's stopping you from moving forward in life?

*Don't you realize that in a race everyone runs, but only one person gets the prize? So run to win!* (1 Corinthians 9:24 NLT)

# 11 Our Examples of Courage

As Nelson Mandela once said, "I learned that courage was not the absence of fear, but the triumph over it. The brave man is not he who does not feel afraid, but he who conquers that fear." One of the greatest examples we have of courage and bravery in America is found in our police officers, fire fighters, and first responders. Today, we remember and honor them as well as the lives lost during the terror attacks in 2001. These warriors allowed courage and strength to mark them that day, and they will be forever remembered for that. They showed us what it looks like to stare fear in the face and command it to stand down. May we use their courage as inspiration for our lives.

## What brings you courage?

*Be strong and of a good courage, fear not, nor be afraid of them: for the Lord thy God, he it is that doth go with thee; he will not fail thee, nor forsake thee.* (Deuteronomy 31:6 KJV)

# When You Make a Mistake

Mistakes happen. Just ask the Coca-Cola Corporation. A few decades ago after 99 years of keeping the same winning recipe for their soda, Coca-Cola executives decided to change Coke's flavor. You see, Pepsi-Cola had started to eat into their market share. By 1983, many people preferred the flavor of Pepsi over Coke. The public immediately revolted against Coca-Cola when they changed the soda's flavor. Within three months, Coca-Cola reverted back to the original recipe. By 1986, Coke was outselling Pepsi again. Their story is a good reminder that mistakes are a part of life. It's our job to recognize when we do make a mistake so we can learn from the situation, correct it as necessary, and move on.

> Have you had the opportunity to turn one of your mistakes into a milestone for your future?

*Stalwart walks in step with God; his path blazed by God, he's happy. If he stumbles, he's not down for long; God has a grip on his hand.* (Psalm 37:24 Msg.)

# ⑬ Deal Well With Conflict

Conflict in a relationship is not necessarily a sign of failure. It's normal for two people who come together in marriage or friendship to disagree at some point because they each have a different point of view. Dr. Gary Chapman once said, "Conflicts are not a sign you've married the wrong person. They simply affirm you are human." The way you handle conflict, though, determines whether the relationship will be a source of pain or peace. Remember that the goal of resolving conflict is not victory or defeat. It's reaching a point of understanding and letting go of our need to be right. Conflict happens, but it can be resolved well.

## Does conflict help or hinder your relationships?

*If your brother sins against you, go and tell him his fault, between you and him alone. If he listens to you, you have gained your brother.* (Matthew 18:15 ESV)

#  The Power of Vision

In his book, *Game On*, retired NFL running back Emmitt Smith talked about the power of vision. He stated, "Vision gets the dreams started. Dreaming employs your God-given imagination to reinforce the vision. Both are part of something I believe is absolutely necessary to building the life of a champion, a winner, [and] a person of high character who is consistently at the top of whatever game he or she is in." When Emmitt was a boy, he dreamed about playing football against the best. As you and I know, his dreams became a reality. Imagine your dreams coming true; then let those dreams propel you to your future.

## What is your vision for your life?

*And the Lord answered me, and said, Write the vision, and make it plain upon tables, that he may run that readeth it. For the vision is yet for an appointed time, but at the end it shall speak, and not lie: though it tarry, wait for it; because it will surely come, it will not tarry.* (Habakkuk 2:2–3 KJV)

## 15 Focus on Now

NFL quarterback Tom Brady has much of which to be proud. He took the Patriots to the Super Bowl nine times, of which they won six championships. He has four Super Bowl MVP awards and three league MVP awards. None of this deters his weekly focus during football season. The only game Brady is focused on is the one happening next. He once said, "I don't care about three years ago. I don't care about two years ago. I don't care about last year. The only thing I care about is this week." He understood that you can build on your past and prepare for your future, but you should never forget the importance of living in the now.

In the mess of the past and the excitement of the future, have you forgotten the purpose and passion of the now?

*Give your entire attention to what God is doing right now, and don't get worked up about what may or may not happen tomorrow. God will help you deal with whatever hard things come up when the time comes.* (Matthew 6:34 Msg.)

#  Push Your Limits

Did you know that our minds sometimes limit us more than our bodies do? All of us have limits we have mentally assumed are true for our lives. We're convinced that we cannot, or should not, go beyond these limits. The reality is, being constrained by fear of the unknown or some type of discomfort keeps us living on a low level of success. It's always in our best interests to push beyond our mental limitations and see what lies on the other side. Basketball great Michael Jordan put it this way: "Never say never because limits, like fears, are often just an illusion." I encourage you to push beyond the limits and dare to see what's on the other side.

## What limits you?

*Wherefore seeing we also are compassed about with so great a cloud of witnesses, let us lay aside every weight, and the sin which doth so easily beset us, and let us run with patience the race that is set before us....* (Hebrews 12:1 KJV)

# 17 Rightly Dividing the Word of God

Each day we can contribute to the wellbeing of this world by making the choice to be kind. Kindness not only provides people with safety and encouragement, but kindness reminds others that there is good in this world. Too often we let the chaos around us drive our emotions to a frazzled state as we wonder how we can change nationwide concerns. In turn, that frustration can leak out into our relationships and harm those we love. So don't get lost in trying to fix problems that are clearly outside of your control. Speak up for truth—and then stand firm in choosing kindness for the strangers, family, and friends in your life.

## How can you choose kindness today?

*Study to shew thyself approved unto God, a workman that needeth not to be ashamed, rightly dividing the word of truth.* (2 Timothy 2:15 KJV)

## 18 Never Give Up

After a walk in the woods in the 1940s, Swiss engineer George de Mestral noticed the unique way burrs clung to his pants and his dog's fur. Most people considered the burrs merely a nuisance, but he saw them and wondered if he could recreate their adhesive effect. He spent the next number of years trying to do so. His persistence in research and development paid off; in 1955, he formally patented his invention of the hook-and-loop fastener we all know as Velcro. He embodied what Thomas Edison knew: "The three great essentials to achieve anything worthwhile are, first, hard work; second, stick-to-itiveness; third, common sense."

How's your "stick-to-it" nature?

*By your steadfastness and patient endurance you shall win the true life of your souls.* (Luke 21:19 Amp.)

## 19 The Pathway to the Top

Years ago, a nine-year-old boy who loved watching Tiger Woods play sat down and wrote a letter to the professional golfer. The letter was intended to put Tiger on alert—"I'm coming to get you. This is the beginning. Watch this space." The boy had set his eyes on a big prize: rivaling one of the top golfers in the world. That young boy turned 30 in 2019, and do you want to guess what he is doing? He's at the top of the PGA circuit, doing exactly what he dreamed he'd do. His name is Rory McIlroy. Rory's drive to rival his hero came true thanks to hard work, dedication, and an unwavering focus on his goal. When you pursue your dream with intensity and passion, your dreams will come true too.

## Are you dreaming big enough?

*My ambition has always been to preach the Good News where the name of Christ has never been heard, rather than where a church has already been started by someone else.* (Romans 15:20 NLT)

What's Your Legacy?

William Wilberforce knew slavery needed to end. As an English politician who lived around the turn of the 19th century, he had a fight on his hands. So many people were invested in the profit of the trade, Wilberforce faced an uphill—and potentially impossible—battle that was filled with ridicule and heartache. After endless days, weeks, and years of legal battle, victory came. Three days before he died, Wilberforce heard that slavery was going to be abolished in the British Empire. You may never know how far your influence will reach. Do good, follow your heart, and live well. Let your legacy be created through perseverance and integrity.

How far can you picture your influence reaching?

*Be ye strong therefore, and let not your hands be weak: for your work shall be rewarded.* (2 Chronicles 15:7 KJV)

## Life's Chain of Events

It's easy to think our actions don't impact people, but that's not the case. Consider this scenario: a woman spills coffee on her blouse and has to change shirts. She speeds to get to work on time, and almost gets into an accident. The near accident causes the man driving the other car to have a near panic attack, which causes him to be irritable. His edginess upsets his wife and causes her to question why she married him. Our lives are connected far beyond anything we will ever understand, so let's remember what former baseball player Wade Boggs once stated: "A positive attitude causes a chain of reaction of positive thoughts, events, and outcomes. It is a catalyst and it sparks extraordinary results."

> Are you aware of how your life is interconnected with others?

*We can rejoice, too, when we run into problems and trials, for we know that they help us develop endurance. And endurance develops strength of character, and character strengthens our confident hope of salvation.* (Romans 5:3–4 NLT)

# Never Stop Learning

If you are not willing to learn, no one can help you. If you are determined to learn, no one can stop you. Valuable employees never stop learning. They are always striving to do more effective work in their current position. They have a solid grasp of what their job entails. If they fall short of the mark or recognize their job requirements have changed, they take the initiative to become further educated. Leonardo Da Vinci understood the power of learning. He stated, "Learning is the only thing the mind never exhausts, never fears, and never regrets."

## Have you recognized the value of continuing education?

*Keep hold of instruction; do not let go; guard her, for she is your life.*

(Proverbs 4:13 ESV)

# 23 What Rules You?

What happens when you have aches and pains in the wrong places or are unexpectedly asked to meet with your boss? For many people, unknown situations such as these trigger immediate fear. The "what will happen" question gets answered with negative thoughts and possibilities. As a result, they become drained of their energy, encouragement, and strength. The good news is, negative outcomes are not the only answer to unknown situations. Good things happen too. So instead of letting fear rule your heart, give thought to what could happen if things went better than expected. Circumstances change for the better when you give as much energy to faith as you do your fears.

What is your default reaction when faced with a negative situation: faith or fear?

*For God hath not given us the spirit of fear; but of power, and of love, and of a sound mind.* (2 Timothy 1:7 KJV)

# Absolute Truth Exists

Is it any wonder that America appears to be falling apart at the moral seams? We're living in a nation in which few people believe in the concept of truth—in particular, absolute truth. Americans seem to be running from the idea of right and wrong and replacing it with moral relativism. What you find morally objectionable may be perfectly okay for me, and what I find right may be wrong for someone else. Given many people accept the idea the universe just happened by chance, that shouldn't come as a big surprise. The problem is, they're wrong. There is a God and there are moral absolutes. Truth is not in the eye of the beholder.

> Have you allowed the world's idea
> of truth to permeate your own?

*Jesus saith unto him, I am the way, the truth, and the life: no man cometh unto the Father, but by me.* (John 14:6 KJV)

# 25 His Will Is Always Good

Many people change their theology based on personal experience; however, this perspective misses two key truths. First, experience—whether your own or the experience of someone you know—is a shaky foundation upon which to build your life. Second, faith won't always be understood. Faith holds onto something greater despite uncertainty. As Max Lucado stated, "Faith is not the belief that God will do what you want. It is the belief that God will do what is right." Your prayers won't always be answered as you expect, but that doesn't mean you should stop praying. Your prayers pave a way for God to work His will—and His will is always good.

Are you willing to place your faith in God's goodness, even when you don't understand?

*Trust in the Lord with all your heart; do not depend on your own understanding.*
*Seek his will in all you do, and he will show you which path to take.*
(Proverbs 3:5–6 NLT)

#  Commitment Is Better

Are we becoming a society who can't commit to anything? Studies seem to say so. Sociologists have identified an alarming trend on the American cultural landscape—an unwillingness to commit to anything. Market researcher George Barna stated, "In the process of defining what counts in life, many of us have decided that commitment is not in our best interests." This is tragic because the Bible says, and history has shown, that values like loyalty and faithfulness are tightly tied to succeeding in life. This trend toward non-commitment is one you need to resist if you want to win in life.

## Are you willing to commit?

*Committed and persistent work pays off; get-rich-quick schemes are ripoffs.*
(Proverbs 28:20 Msg.)

## 27 Kindness Impacts the World

Each day we can contribute to the wellbeing of this world by making the choice to be kind. Kindness not only provides people with safety and encouragement, but kindness reminds others that there is good in this world. Too often we let the chaos around us drive our emotions to a frazzled state as we wonder how we can change nationwide concerns. In turn, that frustration can leak out into our relationships and harm those we love. So don't get lost in trying to fix problems that are clearly outside of your control. Speak up for truth—and then stand firm in choosing kindness for the strangers, family, and friends in your life.

## How can you choose kindness today?

*A man who is kind benefits himself, but a cruel man hurts himself.*
(Proverbs 11:17 ESV)

# Communicate on Their Terms

What should you do when a customer, employee, or your children are frustrated with policies you've set in place? Consider changing their perspective by changing how you approach them about their frustrations. Instead of using the phrase "Because I said so," stir in them a reason to listen by showing them clearly how they will benefit from the situation. Maybe it will be a reward or an increase in responsibility. When you let them know the rules in a way where the benefits for them are clear, it takes the focus off you and puts it on them. You'll begin to win in those relationships.

> Are you expecting those under your authority to blindly follow you or have you given them reason in terms they are interested in?

*A word fitly spoken is like apples of gold in a setting of silver.* (Proverbs 25:11 ESV)

# The Light of Your Lifestyle

When you know people who don't yet know the Lord, it can be tempting to try to preach them into heaven. *Maybe they didn't hear the first time; I better tell them again. ... Their actions haven't changed, so I will try a different angle.* Your heart may be right, but most of the time, you won't get the results you want. (When was the last time you listened and responded to someone preaching at you?) Don't lecture your unsaved spouse. Don't preach to your unsaved manager or boss. Live your life by the standard of God's Word. Let God change the life of unbelievers. Your lifestyle can convict others of their sin when you live by the standard of God's Word.

Is there someone in your life who needs the light in your lifestyle to lead them to the Lord?

*Let your light so shine before men, that they may see your good works, and glorify your Father which is in heaven.* (Matthew 5:16 KJV)

#  When Forgiveness Has Truly Happened

A surefire way to activate forgiveness—and forgetting—is to do something to bless people who frustrate you. Write them a note. Treat them to dinner or buy them a cup of coffee. When you bless them, you're doing two things. First, you're making it hard for them to hold a grudge against you. Second, you're changing your heart toward them. Jesus said where a man's treasure is, there his heart is also. When you begin to give them treasures of prayer, time, or finances, then you move your heart toward them. This is how forgiveness is realized in its final outworking. When you can bless someone as freely as you did before the offense occurred, forgiveness has truly happened.

## Do you need to bless someone in your life in order to activate complete forgiveness?

*Most important of all, continue to show deep love for each other, for love covers a multitude of sins.* (1 Peter 4:8 NLT)

OCTOBER

Image • Bryan Flanagan

# Knowledge and Leadership

Knowledge in and of itself doesn't equate itself with power, but utilized knowledge does. The Bible also shows us that knowledge doesn't automatically translate into leadership and influence. Many people make the mistake of equating knowledge and intelligence with leadership ability, but that isn't necessarily the case. Visit any university and you'll find a faculty filled with geniuses who are exercising little or no influence over others. The apostle Paul tells us that knowledge alone leads only to pride.

> Are you relying in what you know to confer leadership and influence?

*Anyone who claims to know all the answers doesn't really know very much.*
(1 Corinthians 8:2 NLT)

# Clear Communication

Communication is the priceless ability to express ideas and goals clearly. The well-known CEO John Gardner defines leadership as "the process of persuasion and example by which an individual induces a group to take action that is in accord with the leader's purposes." Communication skill is the foundation of a leader's ability to persuade. Although few leaders excel at all forms of communication, every leader should be capable of expressing concepts clearly. This is a biblical principle. For example, 1 Corinthians tells us, "So also you, unless you utter speech that is clear, how will it be known what is spoken?"

## Are you speaking clearly as a leader?

*From a wise mind comes wise speech; the words of the wise are persuasive.* (Proverbs 16:23 NLT)

# 3 The Best Marriage Connection

Why do so many marriages wither and die while a few get stronger with each passing year? Couples whose marriages last a lifetime have a vital trait in common—they know each other by the spirit. Some relationships are based upon pure physical attraction. When age begins to take its toll, the relationship falls apart. Other relationships are based upon attraction to soulish things such as personality, intelligence, and temperament. Love that lasts a lifetime is based on knowing each other by the spirit—the real person on the inside. When you love your spouse by the spirit, your relationship will give you both a lifetime of fulfillment.

Have you taken the time to get to know your spouse in a more personal, spiritual way?

*But Ruth replied, "Don't urge me to leave you or to turn back from you. Where you go I will go, and where you stay I will stay. Your people will be my people and your God my God." (Ruth 1:16 KJV)*

# The God-Kind of Wisdom

Time and again, the Bible points out the dangers of division. "A house divided against itself cannot stand" and "How can two walk together unless they be agreed?" These are just a few of the verses that show the vital nature of being skilled in the art of negotiation. Few things have greater impact on your level of influence than your ability to negotiate. According to the Bible, the key to successfully resolving conflicts is the God-kind of wisdom. Get that kind of wisdom and you'll be a world-class negotiator, knowing how to negotiate conflicts every time.

> What kind of wisdom are you employing in your relationships—yours or God's?

*But the wisdom that is from above is first pure, then peaceable, gentle, and easy to be intreated, full of mercy and good fruits, without partiality, and without hypocrisy.* (James 3:17 KJV)

## 5  Zeal

Perhaps you've heard an athlete whose team has just lost say something like this: "They just wanted it more than we did." There's a powerful truth at the heart of that statement. At the end of the day, victory usually comes not to the one with the most talent but rather the one with the most desire. The successful industrialist Charles Buxton once said, "Experience shows that success is due less to ability than to zeal. The winner is he who gives himself to his work, body and soul." In the Bible, the power of desire to fuel achievement is consistently stated.

> How bad do you want the dreams
> God has put in your heart?

*Looking for that blessed hope, and the glorious appearing of the great God and our Saviour Jesus Christ; Who gave himself for us, that he might redeem us from all iniquity, and purify unto himself a peculiar people, zealous of good works.*
(Titus 2:13–14 KJV)

# 6 Excellence

The Greek philosopher Ovid said, "There is no excellency without difficulty." He was right. Following the path of least resistance always leads to mediocrity. The way to true excellence is much harder. Perhaps that's why it is so rarely traveled these days. One of the primary challenges every leader must face is the need to inspire others to excellence. Throughout the Bible, great leaders motivated others by the example they set themselves. Those who look to you for leadership will take their cues from you. Standards are transmitted from the top.

## What standards of excellence are you imparting to those around you?

*Finally then, brethren, we request and exhort you in the Lord Jesus, that as you received from us instruction as to how you ought to walk and please God (just as you actually do walk), that you excel still more.* (1 Thessalonians 4:1 NASB)

Biblical Wisdom

How would you like a free facelift this morning? Listen to the words of King Solomon in Ecclesiastes 8:1. "Wisdom brightens a man's face and changes its hard appearance." That's right, wisdom can make you better looking! Seriously though, nothing can do more to make you a winner in life than wisdom, and nowhere on earth will you find a better source of wisdom than the Bible. There, you'll find keys to financial increase, raising children with character, and keys to promotion at work. You can be a wiser person and, as an added benefit, get a brighter face in the process.

> Are you taking advantage of the wisdom the Bible has to offer you?

*Who is as the wise man? and who knoweth the interpretation of a thing? a man's wisdom maketh his face to shine, and the boldness of his face shall be changed.* (Ecclesiastes 8:1 KJV)

# Keep Away From Covetousness

When we pray, we often have a specific idea in mind of when our prayer should be answered. If our timeline isn't met, it's easy to get frustrated. What many people don't realize is that one definition of contentment is "without covetousness." If you covet something, your hopes for happiness rest on having that particular thing. If your happiness lies in anything but your relationship with the Lord—even if it's a good thing—you are coveting it and will not get it by the hand of God. True contentment comes from a sense of inward sufficiency in knowing that your hope is in the Lord, not in your circumstances.

Are you content while waiting for your answer to prayer?

*And he said to them, "Take care, and be on your guard against all covetousness, for one's life does not consist in the abundance of his possessions."* (Luke 12:15 ESV)

## 9  Think Like a Winner

Everyone wants to win in life—but a lot of people find themselves losing more often than they are winning. These people often live with a negative, defeatist mentality. Because of that, they are defeated in life. Negative thinking robs your positive expectation for the future. If you think about how badly your friend beat you at ping pong, I guarantee you'll get whipped again during the second game. If you're worried you'll never have enough to pay the bills, you'll find yourself stuck financially. That's why Zig Ziglar said, "Positive thinking will let you do everything better than negative thinking will." So remove the vision of defeat from your life and begin to think like a winner. Your life will turn around as a result.

Are you focused on your past
or on your future?

*I believe that I shall look upon the goodness of the Lord in the land of the living!*
*Wait for the Lord; be strong, and let your heart take courage; wait for the Lord!*
(Psalm 27:13–14 ESV)

# Become a Recruiter

Jesus not only inspired others; He enlisted them in the cause. He didn't just teach them, He enrolled them. Being an effective recruiter is one of the leadership secrets of Jesus. "Follow me" was His frequent invitation to those He encountered. It's one thing to make a good sales presentation. It's another to have the courage to ask for the business. Jesus never failed to ask for the order. Sometimes leaders get so excited about communicating the vision that they forget to sign anyone up to pursue it.

## How effective are you in enrolling others in your vision?

*And he saith unto them, Follow me, and I will make you fishers of men.*
(Matthew 4:19 KJV)

## ⑪ Fervently Expect

If you knew that your prayers would be answered tomorrow, what would you do today? You'd be excited for tomorrow to come. That's exactly the type of expectation God wants you to have. In Philippians 1:19–20, Paul wrote "For I know that this shall turn to my salvation through your prayer, and the supply of the Spirit of Jesus Christ according to my earnest expectation...." Paul was in jail with a death sentence over his head, yet he knew it was subject to change because of what he expected. As a result, he was able to be content. The power of positive expectation will create that same sense of contentment within you.

### What do you expect tomorrow will bring?

*The aspirations of good people end in celebration; the ambitions of bad people crash.* (Proverbs 10:28 Msg.)

# Giving

If you give away a hundred dollars, are you a hundred dollars poorer? Your answer says something about your basic assumptions. There's no question about it, America is a nation of givers. It is estimated that America has more than eight hundred thousand nonprofit organizations that are donor supported. The tendency to give to such organizations is uniquely American. No other people on earth willingly forfeit as much of their earnings to charitable endeavors. In lean times and good, almost two-thirds of all adults make a financial contribution to a nonprofit organization or church in a typical month. It seems most of us have discovered what the Bible teaches: Giving doesn't diminish us; it increases us.

## What is your attitude toward giving?

*Give, and it shall be given unto you; good measure, pressed down, and shaken together, and running over, shall men give into your bosom. For with the same measure that ye mete withal it shall be measured to you again.* (Luke 6:38 KJV)

## 13 Be Careful of Perfection

When Jeff Bezos launched Amazon.com, he wasn't prepared for the overwhelming response he received. He had to quickly expand to a new facility where he and his staff spent many nights packing orders on their hands and knees. One night Jeff overheard his employees commenting on how their bodies ached from kneeling on the concrete floor. He stated, "You know what we need? Knee pads!" The person who heard him looked at him dumbfoundedly and replied, "What we need is packing tables." The next day they purchased packing tables and productivity increased dramatically. The lesson is, you don't have to have everything perfect before you pursue an idea. Start with what you know and improve as you go.

Are you willing to follow through on an idea even before it is perfect?

*A slack hand causes perfection, but the hand of the diligent makes rich.*
(Proverbs 10:4 ESV)

**14** Let the New Propel You Forward

Every time you encounter something new, you are faced with a decision. Will that situation become a learning opportunity or will it become a difficulty? Winston Churchill once said, "A pessimist sees the difficulty in every opportunity; an optimist sees the opportunity in every difficulty." New situations may intimidate you or trigger feelings of inadequacy, but that doesn't mean you should run the other way. You can embrace new situations as an opportunity to learn. You may not yet have the answer you need, but it will come to you as you move forward. So don't let the new intimidate you. Instead, let it inspire you to grow.

How do you approach the new?

*Be strong and courageous. Do not fear or be in dread of them, for it is the Lord your God who goes with you. He will not leave you or forsake you.*
(Deuteronomy 31:6 ESV)

## 15  Serve

Did you know that life is like a game of tennis? The one who "serves" well, seldom loses. Go to any bookstore and you're sure to find a large section labeled Self-Help or Success. Take a closer look and you'll find scores, even hundreds, of books that claim to show you how to get ahead in life. As you look through them, you'll find that many contain a common principle: "If you want to lead, you must learn to serve. Promotion comes through service to others." What these modern success gurus have discovered has been in the Bible all along. Jesus said, "He who would be the greatest among you must be the servant of all." Service. It's an identifying mark of a winner.

### How's your serve?

*And he sat down, and called the twelve, and saith unto them, If any man desire to be first, the same shall be last of all, and servant of all.* (Mark 9:35 KJV)

Train Up Others

The highest form of leadership is the kind that duplicates itself. Wise leaders are constantly cultivating leadership skills in the people around them. This is a truth that has been stated in much of the literature on leadership, but the principle originated in the Bible. Today it's called "mentoring." In the Bible it is referred to as "discipleship." The Bible makes it clear that each person is to exert as much positive influence as possible and to teach others to do the same.

As a leader, what are you doing to create an atmosphere in which new leaders can develop?

*And the Lord has given both him and Oholiab son of Ahisamach, of the tribe of Dan, the ability to teach their skills to others.* (Exodus 35:34 NLT)

# 17 No Favorites

Does God play favorites? It's a question you need to know the answer to if you want to draw sound conclusions about how to live your life. A lot of people look around and conclude that God must be partial to some individuals. They seem to do better. Things seem to go their way more often. But according to the Bible, God makes the same opportunities available to everyone. Acts 10:34 says, "God is no respecter of persons." Another translation says, "God does not show favoritism." That means anyone, regardless of their background or position in life, can prosper spiritually, materially, and physically if they'll follow God's principles and do things His way. Never forget, God is an equal opportunity "blesser."

## Have you realized that God doesn't play favorites?

*Then Peter opened his mouth, and said, Of a truth I perceive that God is no respecter of persons: But in every nation he that feareth him, and worketh righteousness, is accepted with him.* (Acts 10:34–35 KJV)

## Embrace Creative Thought

As the organization you work for grows and as society changes, your methods for accomplishing tasks will need to change. Take, for example, the bakery that developed "PSA cakes" in the middle of the coronavirus pandemic. These cakes offered public service announcements such as "Wash your hands" or "Clean and disinfect." They brightened people's days—and kept the bakery from going bankrupt. So don't fall into the trap of assuming that what you've done for years is the best way to do it. Be willing to reinvent and reimagine as time passes.

How can you make room for creativity today?

*The Lord has filled Bezalel with the Spirit of God,*

*giving him great wisdom, ability, and expertise in all kinds of crafts.*

*He is a master craftsman, expert in working with gold, silver,*

*and bronze.  He is skilled in engraving and mounting gemstones*

*and in carving wood.  He is a master at every craft.*

(Exodus 35:31–33 NLT)

#  Listen First

Receptive listening is the willingness to gather information before making judgments. It's a skill that is common in effective leaders. They listen carefully to those who offer ideas. Those who lack this receptive listening trait cause people to feel rejected rather than appreciated and they stifle the flow of good ideas that might help the effort. Effective leaders do two things: they ask questions, and they listen. This makes people like them, respect them, and want to bring them information. Moses, one of the greatest leaders of people in history, consistently displayed the trait of being a receptive listener.

## Are you a receptive listener?

*He who answers a matter before he hears the facts—It is folly and shame to him.* (Proverbs 18:13 Amp.)

#  20    When Silence Can Be Beneficial

Effective communication doesn't always mean more communication. Benjamin Franklin stated it this way: "He who speaks much is much mistaken." One way to simplify your communication is by learning when to keep quiet. Americans like to have an answer to everything—even when they don't know the right thing to say. Speaking without thinking will get you into trouble. Proverbs 10:19 says, "In the multitude of words there wanteth not sin: but he that refraineth his lips is wise." Learn how to simplify your communication by learning what to say as well as when you should be silent.

## Have you learned the art of being silent?

*A prudent man conceals knowledge, but the heart of fools proclaims folly.*
(Proverbs 12:23 ESV)

#  21   Are You Loyal?

Loyalty is so rare these days because we live in a society that does not value personal submission. On the contrary, it teaches that the ideal and highest position a person can attain is complete personal autonomy. If you want to be promoted to a place of leadership, you need to embrace loyalty—the complete, unswerving commitment to seek the best interests of those in authority over you—even when you disagree with the direction they have set. The fact that it is such a rare commodity in our culture makes you all the more valuable when you possess it.

## Do the people around you consider you loyal?

*He who pursues righteousness and loyalty finds life, righteousness, and honor.*
(Proverbs 21:21 NASB)

**22** Work Together to Reach the Top

Does it have to be lonely at the top? Much of the world today views winning as something that is exclusive. In other words, if you win, everyone else has to lose. The Bible says it's possible to achieve a different kind of winning: one that is inclusive rather than exclusive and one that seeks to dominate circumstances, not people. It's the kind of winning that comes from doing things God's way. This way of winning brings health, peace of mind, solid relationships, financial increase, and much more.

Does your view of winning mean climbing over everyone in your path?

*...A body isn't just a single part blown up into something huge. It's all the different-but-similar parts arranged and functioning together.* (1 Corinthians 12:14 Msg.)

**Benefits Are Good**

When Jesus said, "Ask and it shall be given to you," and "Seek and you shall find," He was demonstrating a keystone of His leadership style. He never asked for commitment or sacrifice from others without speaking in terms of benefits. He knew that people are constructed to be more willing to give up something if they can attain something of greater perceived value. Great leaders spell out the benefits of following.

How can you better frame your message in terms of the felt needs and benefits of those you're trying to lead?

*Ask, and it shall be given you; seek, and ye shall find; knock, and it shall be opened unto you: For every one that asketh receiveth; and he that seeketh findeth; and to him that knocketh it shall be opened.* (Matthew 7:7–8 KJV)

**Be Dependable**

We all know people whose only claim to consistency is the fact that their mood is constantly changing. You never know if they will be grumpy, happy, or somewhere in between. People appreciate consistency. It's frustrating—even stressful—when employers don't know if they can depend on someone to finish a job or when friends tell you one thing and do another. The book of Proverbs says, "Reliable friends who do what they say are like cool drinks in sweltering heat." Employers appreciate consistent, good effort. Friends appreciate dependability. Even your family appreciates it when you choose to be consistent.

## Do people consider you dependable?

*Reliable friends who do what they say are like cool drinks in sweltering heat.*
(Proverbs 25:13 Msg.)

Encouraging a Press

The most gifted leaders have the ability to spur people on to greater heights of achievement than they thought possible. Jesus was such a leader. In the New Testament, you constantly find Him exhorting people. "Take up your bed and walk!" "Step out of the boat and join me on the water!" "Have faith and move mountains!" One of the leadership secrets of Jesus is knowing that people need encouragement and support in making a maximum press or effort.

> Are you the type of leader who encourages others to press on to new breakthroughs?

*I have shewed you all things, how that so labouring ye ought to support the weak, and to remember the words of the Lord Jesus, how he said, It is more blessed to give than to receive.* (Acts 20:35 KJV)

# Be Someone to Count on

During the Civil War, one of the Confederacy's most brilliant and successful generals was J.E.B. Stuart. He closed all of his correspondence to Commanding General Robert E. Lee the same way— "Yours to count on." That sums up in four powerful words one of the most important attributes you can cultivate if you want to experience success and promotion on the job. I'm talking about the quality of commitment. We find this truth woven throughout the Bible such as when the book of Proverbs tells us, "A faithful man will abound with blessings."

## Can the Lord count on you?

*But all of you who were faithful to the Lord your God are still alive today— every one of you.* (Deuteronomy 4:4 NLT)

#  27 Don't Assume

Henry Winkler once said, "Assumptions are the termites of relationships." He was absolutely right. Assumptions often cause multiple frustrations within a relationship. Just think of the wife who assumes her husband has given her an unlimited shopping budget, and the husband who assumes his wife knows they can't spend money right now. Or the employee who assumes he understands the new company policy, but doesn't take the time to actually read it. Each of these assumptions will lead to some type of problem that could have been avoided by proper communication. If you assume you know something, be sure you confirm it verbally with the other person. Communicate; never assume.

When you don't know what is going on in a relationship, do you communicate or assume you know the truth?

When Jesus looked out and saw that a large crowd had arrived, he said to Philip, 'Where can we buy bread to feed these people?' He said this to stretch Philip's faith.

He already knew what he was going to do. Philip answered, 'Two hundred silver pieces wouldn't be enough to buy bread for each person to get a piece.' ... Jesus said, 'Make the people sit down.' There was a nice carpet of green grass in this place.

They sat down, about five thousand of them. Then Jesus took the bread and, having given thanks, gave it to those who were seated. He did the same with the fish. All ate as much as they wanted.

(John 6:5–7, 10–11 Msg.)

#  Admit When You're Wrong

No one likes to have to admit they were wrong, but a major key to finding happiness on the job is the willingness to say, "Hey, I made a mistake." Proverbs 28:13 says, "He who conceals his transgressions will not prosper, but he who confesses and forsakes them will find compassion." Be honest about your mistakes. Becoming known around the office as a person who is willing to own up to mistakes instead of pointing the finger at others, will give you credibility and earn you the respect and trust of those with whom you work... and you'll be happier on the job.

> Do you run and hide when you make a mistake or do you own up to what went wrong?

*I acknowledged my sin unto thee, and mine iniquity have I not hid. I said, I will confess my transgressions unto the Lord; and thou forgavest the iniquity of my sin. Selah. (Psalm 32:5 KJV)*

# Will You Be Someone's Hero?

People often narrow-mindedly assign the part of a hero to those with fame, recognition, or lots of money. What they don't realize is that all it takes to be a hero is to put someone else's life before their own. For example, a few years ago, an 88-year-old woman was pushed down onto subway tracks. Everyone on the platform froze in fear—except one man. He jumped onto the tracks, pushed her to safety, and escaped the tracks himself, six seconds before the subway came. This man may normally be considered "average," but on that day, his reaction to ignore fear and rescue this woman made him a hero.

## Are you willing to put others before yourself?

*Those of us who are strong and able in the faith need to step in and lend a hand to those who falter, and not just do what is most convenient for us. Strength is for service, not status. Each one of us needs to look after the good of the people around us, asking ourselves, "How can I help?"* (Romans 15:1–2 Msg.)

Respect Others' Opinions

No matter how close you are to a person, you'll always come across situations where you disagree. Upbringing, cultural background, and previous experiences create unique perspectives of situations; that doesn't mean one person is right and the other is wrong. Truth has a lot of different sides to it. The greatest challenge is coming to appreciate other people's perspectives. Most of us are so concerned with promoting and defending our point of view that we never make an effort to see why others view a situation differently. Understanding the way others see the point of disagreement is the first step in successfully communicating a solution to that problem.

Are you able to see past your opinions to appreciate other people's perspectives and what they bring to a situation?

*Do not seek revenge or bear a grudge against one of your people, but love your neighbor as yourself. I am the Lord.* (Leviticus 19:18 NIV)

# 31 Be Selfless

Probably one of the most destructive forces within a relationship can be summed up in one little word: self. Selfishness is an ugly characteristic that can crop up continually in our lives if we're not careful. It's easy to spot selfishness in others, but more difficult to see it in ourselves. C.S. Lewis stated it well when he said, "Selfishness has never been admired." If you find yourself throwing a pity party, judging others, or focusing solely on what you want, I encourage you to take a step back. Find perspective by choosing to bless someone else. As much as you think it might, the world does not revolve around you—but you can make it a better place when you choose to focus on others, rather than on yourself.

## Is your focus stuck on yourself?

*Don't be concerned for your own good but for the good of others.*
(1 Corinthians 10:24 NLT)

NOVEMBER

# 1 Include God in Your Voting

The year was 1787 and the convention assembled to draft a constitution for this new "United States of America" was hopelessly deadlocked and on the verge of dissolving. Then the aging and revered Ben Franklin arose to speak. He said, "Sir, the longer I live, the more convincing proofs I see of this truth: that God governs in the affairs of man. And if a sparrow cannot fall to the ground without His notice, is it probable that an empire can rise without His aid?" Then he called the delegates to prayer. That moment represented the turning point of the convention that produced our Constitution. Franklin wisely recognized that our country needed God's help if it was to survive. May we have the same wisdom.

Are you keeping God in America through your prayers and your voting?

*I call heaven and earth to witness against you today, that I have set before you life and death, blessing and curse. Therefore choose life, that you and your offspring may live.* (Deuteronomy 30:19 ESV)

#  Wisdom

Are you a "wise" person? I hope so. According to the Bible, wisdom is one of the most powerful and life-enriching traits any person can possess. True wisdom is a rare commodity in our culture today, but listen to what Proverbs chapter three has to say about its value: "...she is more profitable than silver and yields better returns than gold. She is more precious than rubies; nothing you desire can compare with her. Long life is in her right hand; in her left hand are riches and honor. Her ways are pleasant ways, and all her paths are peace." Want to be wise? The limitless wisdom of God is available to all.

## Are you mining the Bible for the commodity more precious than gold?

*The heart of the discerning acquires knowledge, for the ears of the wise seek it out.* (Proverbs 18:15 NIV)

# The Bible Will Stabilize America

Imagine yourself stranded in a life raft on a cloudy night in the middle of Lake Superior. With no lights in sight, how would you know which direction to begin paddling? You wouldn't, of course. You'd have no fixed standards by which to chart your course. That precisely is the condition of our nation today. Having forgotten the principles that guided our forefathers, we're a people spiritually adrift. Almost 60 years ago, we, as a culture, embarked on the wholesale rejection of God and His Word, hanging a "Not Welcome" sign to Judeo-Christian concepts. In doing so, we tossed aside the moral compass by which any great nation must steer. Now our political leaders grasp in vain for solutions to society's problems. Let's start charting a course for a brighter future. Let's once again steer by the stars of God's truth.

How would the principles of the Bible positively affect America?

*Choose for your tribes wise, understanding, and experienced men, and I will appoint them as your heads.* (Deuteronomy 1:13 ESV)

# Don't Worry; Be Happy

Have you ever found yourself worrying about things you can't change? You're worried your kid won't make friends at school or your teenager won't be home by curfew. You're worried your boss won't give you a raise or your football team will never win the Super Bowl. Whether the "problem" you face is big or small, no amount of worry will ever change circumstances. In fact, the only thing worry does is exhaust you. Corrie ten Boom stated it well when she said, "Worry does not empty tomorrow of its sorrow, it empties today of its strength."

## Are you taking your cares or giving them to God?

*Don't worry about anything; instead, pray about everything. Tell God what you need, and thank him for all he has done. Then you will experience God's peace, which exceeds anything we can understand. His peace will guard your hearts and minds as you live in Christ Jesus.* (Philippians 4:6–7 NLT)

# 5 America's Roots

"A city upon a hill... a light to the world." That's the way the first Puritan settlers in New England saw the new land they were pioneering. The diaries, letters, and charters of the first American colonists paint a clear and vivid picture. They believed that God had led them to this new land in order to show the world how a society based upon God's Word and governed by His love would work. They came to this land filled with a sense of divine destiny—a firm belief that the nation they were founding would send the Gospel message forth to all the world. And although few Americans today realize it, they were right. America is, and always has been, the source of the vast majority of the world's missionary and charitable activity. If we don't rediscover our spiritual roots, however, that legacy is in danger.

## What do you see as America's spiritual roots?

*Blessed is the nation whose God is the Lord; and the people whom He hath chosen for his own inheritance.* (Psalm 33:12 KJV)

# 6 Silence Is Golden

When we don't want to deal with our personal weaknesses, we often surround ourselves with the noise around us. It's as though we prefer listening to other people's conversations rather than the voice in our own head... and here's why: when we stop the flow of information into our heads and simply sit still, that silence amplifies our flaws. Our weaknesses surface and we feel less than ideal. However, that silence is the path to dealing with weakness... for without taking time to identify your weakness, you'll never be able to improve. Silence stops you from simply justifying your beliefs and, instead, challenges you to find your weaknesses and improve them.

## Will you take the time to be silent today?

*For God alone, O my soul, wait in silence, for my hope is from him.*
(Psalm 62:5 ESV)

# 7 Pray for America

Some say America's best days are behind her, that our nation is in an irreversible state of decline. Some believe the American Dream is a thing of the past. However, I have good news for you. The American Dream isn't dead yet. There is still hope for it. If we as a people will begin to return to our spiritual roots—to the biblical ideals and concepts that made this nation great—the Dream will once again begin to stir in the hearts of the people of this country. More importantly, we'll rouse the sleeping giant God brought forth more than 200 years ago to be a light to the world. We'll not only fulfill the American Dream; we'll fulfill God's dream for America.

## Are you doing your part to ensure America obeys God?

*If my people, which are called by my name, shall humble themselves, and pray, and seek my face, and turn from their wicked ways; then will I hear from heaven, and will forgive their sin, and will heal their land.* (2 Chronicles 7:14 KJV)

# Embrace Transparency

Is the silent person truly strong? Not necessarily. Real-life heroes are courageous enough to be honest. They're brave enough to risk rejection and take their defenses down. These real winners are not afraid to be transparent about what's in their hearts. They know that people must know what's truly in your heart before they can be sure you're someone they can trust. Throughout the Bible, God willingly disclosed His heart so His people could learn to trust Him. Trust can't occur without a careful measure of self-disclosure.

### Do you have the courage to be more transparent with those around you?

*Long ago God spoke many times and in many ways to our ancestors through the prophets. And now in these final days, he has spoken to us through his Son....*
(Hebrews 1:1–2 NLT)

# 9   Change Starts With You

It's always easier to see someone else's shortcomings than it is your own. That's why one of the biggest barriers to resolving problems in relationships is the belief that you can somehow change the other person. King David wrote these words in the 139th Psalm: "Search me, O God, and know my heart; try me and know my anxious thoughts. And see if there be any hurtful way in me." David had the sense to know that he was the only one he could change and the wisdom to ask God what needed changing. Do the same and you'll be on your way to winning in your relationships.

> Who do you expect to change in your relationships: the other person or you?

*Don't pick on people, jump on their failures, criticize their faults— unless, of course, you want the same treatment. That critical spirit has a way of boomeranging.* (Matthew 7:1–2 Msg.)

# Make Integrity Your Only Option

The lines surrounding truth have blurred to become relative to each situation, opinion, and experience. This purposeful cover-up of truth may be "socially acceptable," but I challenge you to consider a better way to live. You see, socially acceptable does not equal personally beneficial. Neither does "fast" or "easy" equate with "best." Choices made with integrity are tough, but they will always lead to success in the long run. As Zig Ziglar stated, "With integrity, you have nothing to fear, since you have nothing to hide. With integrity, you will do the right thing, so you will have no guilt." Integrity will always pay off.

Are you willing to stand up for truth regardless of what society thinks?

*Having a good conscience; that, whereas they speak evil of you, as of evildoers, they may be ashamed that falsely accuse your good conversation in Christ.*
(1 Peter 3:16 KJV)

# 11 Thanking Our Military

Every year, we have a few days set aside to honor those who currently serve or have served in our nation's military, but that shouldn't keep us from praying for them and serving them throughout the year. These men and women have invested their lives in protecting our nation and securing our freedom. I can't tell you how special that is in my heart and, I believe, in the heart of God. If someone you know has a family member deployed, extend them a helping hand. Make sure their needs are met. Pray for their peace and protection, and thank them for their service to our country. Our military families should not have to serve alone. Let's stand with them.

## What can you do to thank our military?

*May the Lord, the God of Israel, under whose wings you have come to take refuge, reward you fully for what you have done.* (Ruth 2:12 NLT)

#  Work With Enthusiasm

Ralph Waldo Emerson once said, "Nothing great was ever achieved without enthusiasm." Wise leaders know the truth of that statement and look for great attitudes in those they promote. The people most likely to be elevated to positions of leadership are those with a "great attitude." I once read that real leadership has less to do with "position" than it does with "disposition." Whiners, complainers, pouters, faultfinders, and naysayers don't have the disposition for which leaders look. Winners, on the other hand, say, "We can do it!"

## What type of attitude do you have on the job?

*Do everything without complaining and arguing, so that no one can criticize you. Live clean, innocent lives as children of God, shining like bright lights in a world full of crooked and perverse people.* (Philippians 2:14–15 NLT)

# 13 Misconceptions Cloud Communication

When two people disagree, does it mean that one of them is being irrational? Not necessarily. Two intelligent people can look at a set of facts and draw entirely different conclusions. How is that possible? They start with different sets of "presuppositions." All the conclusions we draw in life and all the decisions we make rest upon some basic assumptions. If those assumptions are accurate, our conclusions are sound. The problem is, many people live their lives holding faulty assumptions. At an early age, parents, teachers, and even ministers can plant misconceptions in us that we carry the rest of our lives.

Have you learned how to identify and deal with misconceptions in your life?

...*[love] beareth all things, believeth all things, hopeth all things, endureth all things.* (1 Corinthians 13:7 KJV)

**Take Initiative**

We all have dreams in our hearts. The big question is, how are we supposed to attain those dreams? The road to accomplishing your dreams is not paved with good intentions. It's paved with action. As the common saying goes, "Do not wait to strike till the iron is hot; make it hot by striking." If you have a dream of becoming an artist, the first thing you need to do is pick up a paintbrush and start creating. If you want to become the CEO of a large corporation, do well in school or get your MBA. Talk to people in your field of interest and see what steps they took to achieve success. Never get stuck at good intentions. Put action to your dreams, and step by step, you'll see them become a reality.

Are your aspirations stuck in the dreaming phase or have you acted on what you want for your life?

*Our orders—backed up by the Master, Jesus—are to refuse to have anything to do with those among you who are lazy and refuse to work the way we taught you. ... We showed you how to pull your weight when we were with you, so get on with it. We didn't sit around on our hands expecting others to take care of us. In fact, we worked our fingers to the bone, up half the night moonlighting so you wouldn't be burdened with taking care of us. And it wasn't because we didn't have a right to your support; we did. We simply wanted to provide an example of diligence, hoping it would prove contagious. (2 Thessalonians 3:6–9 Msg.)*

Image • Eastman Childs

# 15 Rest

After six days of brilliant creative work, God did something too few of us ever take time to do. He rested. Studies show that Americans are working more than at any time in our history. Yet God created us with a very real need to recharge our batteries through regular periods of rest and recreation. That's why the fourth commandment is "remember the Sabbath." It was to be a day of rest and refreshing communion with God. And with today's pressurized demands, even more is needed. As author Bob Harrison has written, "Don't just think of relaxation in terms of weekends. Each day carve out little niches of relaxation time to reduce pressure and clear your mind." It's a major key to maintaining your grip on the demands of life.

## Are you taking time to relax and unwind from the pressures of life?

*And on the seventh day God ended his work which he had made; and he rested on the seventh day from all his work which he had made.* (Genesis 2:2 KJV)

## 16 Redeem the Time

American writer Carl Sandburg once said, "Time is the coin of your life. It is the only coin you have, and only you can determine how it will be spent." Since relationships, ministry, and day-to-day tasks are continually clamoring for my time, I choose to set aside time each morning to pray over my day and decide what it should look like. Pre-planning my day—and allowing time for unexpected items—allows me to manage my time in a way that contributes to God's plan for my life. I encourage you to make time management a priority as well. When you do, you'll find yourself successfully accomplishing not only your daily tasks but also your long-term life goals.

Have you adjusted your schedule to make time with God a priority?

...see then that ye walk circumspectly, not as fools, but as wise, redeeming the time, because the days are evil. (Ephesians 5:15–16 KJV)

# Risk Taking

It's been said that a turtle only makes progress when he sticks his neck out. That's certainly true for organizations. Without risk, there can be no significant increase. That's why, when it comes to creating an atmosphere in your company in which leaders can develop, it is important to teach others to take managed, calculated risks. John Akers once said, "The people who are playing it totally safe are never going to have either the fun or the reward of the people who decide to take some risk, stick it out, and do it differently."

Do the potential leaders around you perceive that risk-taking is encouraged?

*Have not I commanded thee? Be strong and of a good courage; be not afraid, neither be thou dismayed: for the Lord thy God is with thee whithersoever thou goest.* (Joshua 1:9 KJV)

# 18 Don't Be Defensive

How many times have you heard someone in the middle of a heated discussion say, "Don't get defensive"? When someone feels like they are being verbally attacked, it's perfectly natural to throw up a wall of defense that shuts off the flow of communication. One of the premier marks of a winning communicator is the ability to avoid defensiveness and to keep others from feeling so threatened that they become defensive. James 3:2 in the Bible says it this way: "If any man offend not in word, the same is a perfect—or mature—man, and able also to bridle the whole body." Be confident enough not to become defensive and be sensitive enough not to offend, and you'll enjoy relationships that are more harmonious, more productive, and more rewarding.

## How do you respond when you feel attacked?

*...It does not demand its own way. It is not irritable, and it keeps no record of being wronged.* (1 Corinthians 13:5 NLT)

**19** ## What Are You Blessed With?

"Count your blessings." It's become a trite cliché for most Americans but it's a powerful prescription for putting things in perspective and it's particularly appropriate to remind ourselves during the month we celebrate Thanksgiving. With all the irritations and challenges life offers, it's easy to get so focused on our problems that we lose sight of all the good things for which we have to be thankful. According to the Bible, those good things come from God. So why not let the month of Thanksgiving serve as a reminder to count your blessings. It will change your outlook.

> Which is more prominent in your mind throughout the day: your difficulties or your blessings?

*Every good gift and every perfect gift is from above, and cometh down from the Father of lights, with whom is no variableness, neither shadow of turning.* (James 1:17 KJV)

# The Attitude of Gratitude

Author Alan Cohen once stated, "Gratitude, like faith, is a muscle. The more you use it, the stronger it grows, and the more power you have to use it on your behalf. If you do not practice gratefulness, its benefaction will go unnoticed, and your capacity to draw on its gifts will be diminished." He's right. Gratefulness is a strength-building exercise that is not used enough. Being thankful takes your perspective off negative things and deliberately puts them on the positive. As Cohen continued, "To be grateful is to find blessings in everything. This is the most powerful attitude to adopt, for there are blessings in everything."

## Have you exercised your gratitude muscle today?

*Be careful for nothing; but in every thing by prayer and supplication with thanksgiving let your requests be made known unto God. And the peace of God, which passeth all understanding, shall keep your hearts and minds through Christ Jesus.* (Philippians 4:6–7 KJV)

**Give Thanks**

In 1863, President Lincoln declared a national day of thanksgiving. He wrote, "We have been the recipients of the choicest bounties of heaven. We have been preserved in peace and prosperity. We have grown in numbers, wealth, and power, as no other nation has ever grown. But we have forgotten God. We have imagined that all these blessings were produced by some superior wisdom and virtue of our own. Intoxicated by our own success, we have become too proud to pray to the God that made us." May that not be so for us this year. May we instead take time to recognize God's gracious hand in our lives.

How can you ensure that this Thanksgiving is a time of thanking God for all He has done?

*Enter into his gates with thanksgiving, and into his courts with praise: be thankful unto him, and bless his name. For the Lord is good; his mercy is everlasting; and his truth endureth to all generations.* (Psalm 100:4–5 KJV)

## Where Good Ideas Come From

It didn't take me too long in ministry before I discovered that 99% of the good ideas weren't my own. Most good ideas came from somebody the Lord had sent to me, and the only way I could extract those good ideas from them was by being willing to yield to reason. That meant putting aside my great idea and listening to what others had to say. The same is true for you and those around you. When others know that their opinions are important to you and when they know you care about what they think, you will make headway in influencing their lives. Take time to listen to the ideas of others. As you do, you'll find that they'll be more willing to listen to yours.

Are you listening to the ideas the people around you have?

*If you quit listening, dear child, and strike off on your own, you'll soon be out of your depth.* (Proverbs 19:27 Msg.)

#  Why a Budget Is Important

Nobody likes the idea of having a limit on spending, but a budget helps you reach one of the most basic goals of financial management: don't spend more than you make. With the credit cards and charge accounts available nowadays, it is easy to spend money you don't have. If your expenditures exceed your income, you have one of two options available: increase your income or reduce your expense. Proverbs 27:23 says, "Know well the face of your flocks; and pay attention to your herds." You need to know well what's happening with your family's income and manage it appropriately. A budget helps you recognize where your money is going, but it won't help you financially unless you follow it.

## Have you set up a budget for yourself and family?

*But don't begin until you count the cost. For who would begin construction of a building without first calculating the cost to see if there is enough money to finish it?* (Luke 14:28 NLT)

# Pray

The unexpected twists and turns of life can often cause unwelcome amounts of stress. We try as hard as we can to make our lives return to the way we want things to be. What we can so easily forget is that God is at work behind the scenes to bring His will to pass in our lives. The Bible promises us that God will never leave us nor forsake us. That means, in our darkest hour, He is by our side waiting to help. God is bigger, stronger, and more knowledgeable than you, so even though you may not understand it, your best course of action will always be to ask for the Lord's help.

## Are you willing to put aside your pride and pray?

*Yea, though I walk through the valley of the shadow of death, I will fear no evil: for thou art with me; thy rod and thy staff they comfort me. Thou preparest a table before me in the presence of mine enemies: thou anointest my head with oil; my cup runneth over.* (Psalm 23:4–5 KJV)

#  Love

What's the one thing in our society we talk about the most and understand the least? Of all the concepts in the English language, none is as overused and under comprehended than "love." We use the word so frequently it has become meaningless. You need to know that it's not meaningless to God. When He talks about love, He means something very important. We find a great definition of love in the thirteenth chapter of 1 Corinthians. It says, "Love is patient, love is kind. It does not envy, it does not boast, it is not proud. It is not rude, it is not self-seeking, it is not easily angered, it keeps no record of wrongs. Love does not delight in evil but rejoices with the truth. It always protects, always trusts, always hopes, always perseveres." That's the God-kind of love. As you begin to love like that, your relationships will never be the same.

Is the God kind of love a
part of your life?

*Though I speak with the tongues of men and of angels, and have not charity, I am become as sounding brass, or a tinkling cymbal. And though I have the gift of prophecy, and understand all mysteries, and all knowledge; and though I have all faith, so that I could remove mountains, and have not charity, I am nothing. And though I bestow all my goods to feed the poor, and though I give my body to be burned, and have not charity, it profiteth me nothing.* (1 Corinthians 13:1–3 KJV)

# Attitude Check

Your attitude is either your best friend or your worst enemy, your greatest asset, or your greatest liability. The familiar saying that "attitude determines altitude" is absolutely true. John Maxwell has called attitude, "the eye of your soul. If your attitude is negative, then you see things negatively. If it's positive, then you see things positively." Harvard psychologist William James wrote, "The greatest discovery of my generation is that a human being can alter his life by altering his attitudes of mind." Throughout the Bible, God shows us that our attitudes greatly affect our quality of life. On numerous occasions the apostle Paul exhorts us to keep our attitudes humble, positive, and pure. For those who do, the Bible promises peace, increase, and fulfilling relationships.

## What's your attitude like?

*But my servant Caleb has a different attitude than the others have. He has remained loyal to me, so I will bring him into the land he explored. His descendants will possess their full share of that land.* (Numbers 14:24 NLT)

#  Get Rid of the Clutter

Unfinished business is a common source of stress for many people. I'm talking about the pile of papers next to your computer, the unanswered voicemails on your phone, and the to-do list that hasn't yet been conquered. Simple tasks left undone because of some excuse add unnecessary stress to already busy lives. Becoming a finisher doesn't always take that long. If you take five minutes to organize your mail or return a phone call, you'll be one step closer to a clean desk and less stress. Daily tasks are easy to push aside in favor of the bigger projects on your plate, but they can clutter your life when ignored.

## Have you let unfinished business clutter your life?

*Our people have to learn to be diligent in their work so that all necessities are met (especially among the needy) and they don't end up with nothing to show for their lives.* (Titus 3:14 Msg.)

# Let Offense Roll Off Your Back

"One of my goals is to become more difficult to offend." Jon Acuff's goal is one that would benefit many. Offense has torn apart many relationships. You see, too many people place the responsibility for offense on the person who offended—but just because someone said something offensive doesn't mean you have to be offended. You can choose the path of kindness and unconditional love. The apostle Paul put it this way: "Love is not easily provoked." The next time you have the opportunity to be offended, I challenge you to avoid dwelling on the offense. Choose instead to let love stick in that relationship and let offense roll off your back

## Which have you been letting stick in your life: offense or love?

*Good sense makes one slow to anger, and it is his glory to overlook an offense.* (Proverbs 19:11 ESV)

## 29  Graceful Speech

Have you ever wished you were the type of person who always knew the right thing to say? You probably know someone who always seems to have just the right words at just the right time. Most people aren't born with that gift. It's cultivated and developed. And according to the Bible, it's something you acquire by adding "grace" and "seasoning" to your speech. Colossians 4:6 says, "Let your speech always be with grace, seasoned, as it were, with salt, so that you may know how you should respond to each person." Effective, timely, gracious communication gives you the right word for every occasion.

### What are you speaking today?

*Do not let any unwholesome talk come out of your mouths, but only what is helpful for building others up according to their needs, that it may benefit those who listen.* (Ephesians 4:29 NIV)

#  When You Shouldn't Trust

Imagine for a moment you and your spouse were going out of town for the weekend. Would you ask your new neighbors to watch your children? Of course not. Since you haven't spent time with them, you don't know how much you can entrust to their care. You remain kind and believe the best about them as you watch their lives unfold. Then you'll see where your level of trust can be placed. In the same way, when you make a decision to forgive someone who has wronged you, you shouldn't necessarily decide to trust them right away. If that person broke your trust, let time pass so trust can be rebuilt. Trust comes when you no longer have a lack of knowledge about a person's level of integrity and commitment to the Word. Remember, forgiveness and love are granted, but trust is built.

## Are you trusting someone who has hurt you too quickly?

*But I say unto you, Love your enemies, bless them that curse you, do good to them that hate you, and pray for them which despitefully use you, and persecute you;* (Matthew 5:44 KJV)

DECEMBER

Image • Josh Hild

BLUE LINE

METRO

2198

# 1 Tell the Truth

Our society has desensitized us to the need for truth. As a result, it's easy to begin dealing in lies, usually on a subconscious level. We think, "If he's going to shade the truth, then I will too" or "I can't let her get ahead of me or else I'll get behind the power curve." God makes truth a major issue throughout the Word. Proverbs 12:22 says, "Lying lips are [an] abomination to the Lord: but they that deal truly are his delight." Liars will never be entrusted with any significant degree of responsibility. If you're ever going to win in life, you must grow beyond the tendencies to shade the truth and make complete truth a priority in your communication.

## Is truth continually present in your communication?

*But speaking the truth in love, may grow up into him in all things, which is the head, even Christ:* (Ephesians 4:15 KJV)

# 2  The Real Celebration

What words do you associate with the Christmas season? If you're like some Americans, the words that come to mind might be pressure, stress, crowds, demands, expenses, or debt. Contrast that picture with the one painted by the true meaning of Christmas—the one found in the Bible. There you'll find words like peace, wonder, good news, and great joy. Do you see how far we've drifted from the qualities that make Christmas meaningful? I've got good news for you. It's not too late to stop and restore the wonder and beauty of Christmas in your home.

## How do you acknowledge and honor the real reason of Christmas at your house?

*For unto you is born this day in the city of David a Saviour, which is Christ the Lord. And this shall be a sign unto you; Ye shall find the babe wrapped in swaddling clothes, lying in a manger. And suddenly there was with the angel a multitude of the heavenly host praising God, and saying, Glory to God in the highest, and on earth peace, good will toward men. (Luke 2:11–14 KJV)*

# ③ Kindness Starts at Home

Altogether too often, family members use each other as proverbial punching bags. They wound with words and push each other's buttons more than they would with other people. They seem to instinctively rely on the statement: "They are family; they have to love me anyway." Your siblings, parents, and spouse are the people you know best. Don't choose to willingly aggravate these relationships just because you can.  Your family should be the people you protect most in life, so work to create a loving, welcoming environment when you are together.

Do you contribute to an encouraging atmosphere at home or does your family get the brunt of your anger?

*Friends love through all kinds of weather, and families stick together in all kinds of trouble.* (Proverbs 17:17 Msg.)

#  The Canvas of Your Mind

Olympian Carl Lewis once stated, "Scientists have proven that it's impossible to long-jump 30 feet, but I don't listen to that kind of talk. Thoughts like that have a way of sinking into your feet." He hit on a basic truth about life: thoughts are integral to success. What you think about the most will dictate where you walk in the future. If you want to be the best at what you do, build a picture of your dreams on the canvas of your mind. The more you think on it, the clearer your vision will become. And remember what Michael Phelps stated: "You can't put a limit on anything. The more you dream, the further you will get."

## What picture is on the canvas of your mind?

*Finally, brethren, whatsoever things are true, whatsoever things are honest, whatsoever things are just, whatsoever things are pure, whatsoever things are lovely, whatsoever things are of good report; if there be any virtue, and if there be any praise, think on these things.* (Philippians 4:8 KJV)

# 5 Own It

We're living in a day in which fewer and fewer people seem willing to take responsibility for anything, including their own lives. One of the leadership secrets of Jesus was His willingness to shoulder responsibility and make it His own. This is the hallmark of great leaders. They take a vision, or mandate, and own it. It shows in everything they do.

Is the way you're currently handling the vision or mandate you've been given showing that you've taken ownership of it?

*Arise, for it is your duty, and we are with you. Be strong and brave and do it.*
(Ezra 10:4 Amp.)

December

# 6 Humility

King Solomon was one of the wisest men who ever lived. In Proverbs 18:12 he writes, "Before his downfall a man's heart is proud, but humility comes before honor." Many people have a distorted idea of what humility is. They think you have to consider yourself a no-good worm to be truly humble. That's certainly not the case. True humility doesn't mean having a poor self-image. On the contrary, the kind of humility that brings you honor is the quiet confidence that comes from knowing that your gifts, talents, and your very life itself all come from God.

## Is true humility a part of your life?

*For I say, through the grace given unto me, to every man that is among you, not to think of himself more highly than he ought to think; but to think soberly, according as God hath dealt to every man the measure of faith.* (Romans 12:3 KJV)

# 7  When to Have an Argument

"The thing I hate about an argument is that it always interrupts a discussion." These words by GK Chesterton prove an interesting point. Discussion should be a part of every relationship, for that is how decisions are made, feelings are shared, and resolutions are reached. However, when emotions take over and you begin throwing insults at each other, productivity diminishes greatly and bitterness is given the opportunity to take root. One key to keep this from happening is to avoid having necessary discussions when you are tired, hungry, and upset. In order to properly resolve conflict, postpone the conversation until both parties are in a better frame of mind.

Are you willing to set feelings aside so a resolution can be reached?

*But as he who called you is holy, you also be holy in all your conduct.*
(1 Peter 1:15 ESV)

# Responsiveness

The best leaders aren't merely experts at exercising authority. They have also trained themselves to be "under" authority, as well. You can't have it both ways. You can't expect those you lead to be responsive to your authority if you consistently show a rebellious and independent attitude toward those in authority over you. The Bible has much to say about the importance of submission and honoring authority. It also teaches that you reap what you sow.

If you want to reap greater responsiveness to your leadership, why not try sowing a little more responsiveness to those you serve?

*Obey them that have the rule over you, and submit yourselves: for they watch for your souls, as they that must give account, that they may do it with joy, and not with grief: for that is unprofitable for you. (Hebrews 13:17 KJV)*

# 9 Become an Idea Person

I love to be around people with ideas. It's easy to find people who are experts at seeing the problem. It's the rare and valuable person who always seems to have an idea for the solution. When you examine the qualities of the people most frequently chosen for promotion and leadership, you discover that the vast majority are people who generate lots of new ideas, new thoughts, fresh ways of looking at a situation. Fear keeps most people from training their minds to think creatively and keeps them from putting forth a new idea when they happen to have one. Being a solution-oriented person with lots of ideas will position you for promotion and increase on the job.

## Do you respond to problems with solutions or more problems?

*Do not neglect the gift you have, which was given you by prophecy when the council of elders laid their hands on you.* (1 Timothy 4:14 ESV)

#  Place a Priority on Integrity

Centuries ago, King Solomon penned these words: "Better is a poor man who walks in his integrity than a rich man who is crooked in his ways." In 2010, San Francisco Giants pitcher Jeremy Affeldt lived out these words. A clerical error allowed him to be overpaid $500,000 in his baseball contract. His agent told him, "As your agent, I've got to tell you that legally you can keep it. As a man who represents integrity, I'm saying you should give it back." Affeldt did exactly that: he gave up a "free" half a million dollars so he could keep his integrity.

> Will you follow his example and do the right thing, even when the wrong way looks appealing?

*He that walketh uprightly walketh surely: but he that perverteth his ways shall be known.* (Proverbs 10:9 KJV)

# 11 Pursue Peace

"Peace on earth" is a phrase you hear in many Christmas carols and passages of Scripture. For many, it holds the connotation of peace among all nations—but did you know it can also apply to your own life? The dictionary defines "peace" as "freedom of the mind from annoyance, distraction, or anxiety." It's a place of tranquility or serenity. Now, this type of peace isn't just handed to you. If you want peace in your relationships, you need to be a peacemaker. If you want peace in your finances, follow a budget. If you want peace on the job, actively give 100% every time you clock in. So today I want to remind you that peace can happen in your life, but it's your job to pursue it.

Are you allowing peace to rule in your life?

*Turn away from evil and do good; seek peace and pursue it.* (Psalm 34:14 ESV)

# Dreams Create Momentum

Robert Greenleaf has said, "Nothing much happens without a dream. For something really great to happen, it takes a really great dream." The Bible has a lot to say about dreams, visions, hopes, and desires. It's filled with accounts of men and women who allowed God to paint dreams on the canvases of their hearts. Dreams are the wellspring of passion. They give us direction and point us to lofty heights. They capture the imagination and engage the spirit. They grab us and move us. They are capable of lifting us to new heights and helping us break through our self-imposed limitations. God-given dreams are the seeds of greatness.

Are you allowing the dream God placed in your heart to propel you forward?

*Now unto him that is able to do exceeding abundantly above all that we ask or think, according to the power that worketh in us, Unto him be glory in the church by Christ Jesus throughout all ages, world without end. Amen.*
(Ephesians 3:20–21 KJV)

# ⑬ Attitude During Adversity

Charles Swindoll once said, "Life is 10% what happens to me and 90% how I react to it." I agree. A lot of people get overwhelmed when bad things happen. They think they're a loser or they'll never amount to anything or that God is mad at them. The truth is that adversity is a common experience for everyone who has walked this earth. The Bible states it this way: "No temptation..." That's another way of saying adversity. "...has overtaken you except what is common to mankind." So when hard times come, don't get uptight or point your finger at God. Know, instead, that difficulty can turn around for the better. Remember: The difference between a happy person and a sad one is how you react to adversity when it comes.

## How have you reacted recently when faced with adversity?

*My brethren, count it all joy when ye fall into divers temptations; Knowing this, that the trying of your faith worketh patience. But let patience have her perfect work, that ye may be perfect and entire, wanting nothing.* (James 1:2–4 KJV)

# Put Others First

Ralph Waldo Emerson once said, "There is no limit to what can be accomplished if it doesn't matter who gets the credit." A winning relationship is characterized by humility. Paul writes in Philippians 2:3, "Let nothing be done through strife or vainglory; but in lowliness of mind let each esteem others better than themselves." Being humble doesn't mean that you allow other people to walk all over you, but it does mean that you put their needs and interests before your own. Be humble and you will win in your relationships on a consistent basis.

> ## Who is first in your relationships— you or other people?

*Likewise, ye younger, submit yourselves unto the elder. Yea, all of you be subject one to another, and be clothed with humility: for God resisteth the proud, and giveth grace to the humble. Humble yourselves therefore under the mighty hand of God, that he may exalt you in due time....* (1 Peter 5:5–6 KJV)

## 15 How Can You Grow?

George Washington once said, "We ought not look back unless it is to derive useful lessons from past errors and for the purpose of profiting by dearly bought experience." Washington was right. Looking back is usually a dangerous and unprofitable exercise, but the end of the year is not a bad time to see if any important lessons have been learned. According to the book of Proverbs, a prudent person is one who learns from past errors.

> As you look back on this past year, what lessons have you learned that can make you a better person in the coming year?

*Whoever heeds instruction is on the path to life, but he who rejects reproof leads others astray.* (Proverbs 10:17 ESV)

# The Power of the Tongue

Sarcasm has become a staple in American communication, but sarcastic comments that poke fun at people for the sake of a laugh are weapons that wound others. Realize your tongue is a powerful weapon. Proverbs 18:21 says that life and death are in the power of the tongue. Every time you have a conversation with someone, you are providing words that will bless or words that will hurt. Once those words are spoken, you cannot take them back. If you want to win in your relationships, eliminate sarcasm from your speech and fill your words with blessing.

> Are you speaking words that hurt
> or words that encourage?

*People can tame all kinds of animals, birds, reptiles, and fish, but no one can tame the tongue. ... Sometimes it praises our Lord and Father, and sometimes it curses those who have been made in the image of God. And so blessing and cursing come pouring out of the same mouth. Surely, my brothers and sisters, this is not right!* (James 3:7, 9–10 NLT)

# Don't Manipulate

Whether you realize it or not, everybody exercises some degree of power over other people. When we use our leverage to gain our way, we actually oppress the people around us. Statements like "If you don't do this, then I'll do this" or "You need to do this for me because I've done so much for you" intimidate, manipulate, and ultimately threaten relationships. This is why we should know that the way we conduct ourselves will either generate or diffuse a threat environment. We need to learn to communicate without making people feel threatened or defensive. We can do this by, first of all, taking time to listen, and secondly, being willing to yield to reason. When other people know you care about them, the threat environment is diffused and they will be willing to listen to what you have to say.

## Do you care enough about people to avoid manipulating them?

*...[love] does not insist on its own way....* (1 Corinthians 13:5 ESV)

# Avoid Over Communication

One of the most frequently overlooked communication mistakes leaders make is the tendency to "over-communicate." Over-communication is communication that lacks focus. Some poor communicators sound like an entire newspaper instead of an article focused on a subject. They say a great deal about everything, but when they finish, people ask, "What was the point?" When leaders communicate, less is often more. Maybe that's why the book of Proverbs says, "When there are many words, transgression is unavoidable, but he who restrains his lips is wise."

## Are you making the leadership mistake of over communicating?

*Even a fool who keeps silent is considered wise; when he closes his lips, he is deemed intelligent.* (Proverbs 17:28 ESV)

## 19  Peace at Home

With people running at breakneck speed to get in their holiday parties and gift shopping, "peace on earth" can easily become nothing more than a phrase sung while caroling. But, contrary to what some people's schedules imply, you can let peace be a part of your life—and it starts by learning to say, "No." Consider booking your schedule until it's around 80% full; that way when emergencies arise, you have time to adjust. When you're scheduled to 100 or even 110%, there's no room for peace and the rest of your life will be hard to handle. I encourage you to say "no" at some point during this season so you can say "yes" to peace at home.

What have you been doing to proactively keep peace at home?

*See then that ye walk circumspectly, not as fools, but as wise, redeeming the time, because the days are evil.* (Ephesians 5:15–16 KJV)

#  20    Your Children's Values

Do you know why God chose Abraham, out of all the people on earth, to establish a special relationship? According to the book of Genesis, it was because God knew Abraham would impart values to his children. Imparting character and values to your children is one of the most important and most challenging aspects of parenting. C. Everett Koop once wrote, "Values are the foundation of our character and of our confidence. A person who does not know what he stands for, or what he 'should' stand for, will never enjoy true happiness and success." Parents, you can be sure of one thing— your children are adopting someone's value system. Why not decide today to take the time and effort required to impart a positive one.

## From whom are your children learning their value system?

*The rod and reproof give wisdom: but a child left to himself bringeth his mother to shame.* (Proverbs 29:15 KJV)

# 21 The Miraculous

Seven hundred years before the birth of Christ, the prophet Isaiah made a bold and startling prediction. He wrote, "Behold, a virgin shall conceive, and bear a son, and shall call his name Immanuel." Of all the miraculous events recorded in the Bible, no other has sparked more skepticism than the claim that Jesus was born of a virgin. But is it really that hard to believe that a God whose power is so evident in the beauty and complexity of creation, could move in the life of a girl from Galilee to produce a Son? Isaiah said His name would be Immanuel, meaning "God with us." The true wonder is not that God was able to cause a virgin to conceive, but that He chose to do so as a sacrifice for a sinful, rebellious race.

## Is the miracle of Christmas a reality to you?

*Behold, a virgin shall be with child, and shall bring forth a son, and they shall call his name Emmanuel, which being interpreted is, God with us. (*Matthew 1:23 KJV)

#  Peace Today

Around two thousand years ago, a seemingly ordinary young couple began an extraordinary journey. Mary and Joseph of Nazareth in Galilee started on a trek that would change the course of human history. They embarked upon the road to Bethlehem. You may be thinking, *The Christmas story is very nice, but what does it have to do with me?* The answer is, "Everything." There are some truths hidden there that can absolutely revolutionize your life. Truths that can strengthen your marriage and family; truths that can give you a greater sense of purpose and fulfillment on the job; truths that can bring you personally the "peace on earth" promised by the angels that wonderful night in Bethlehem.

## How have the events of the Christmas story impacted your life?

*And suddenly there was with the angel a multitude of the heavenly host praising God, and saying, Glory to God in the highest, and on earth peace, good will toward men.* (Luke 2:13–14 KJV)

## 23 Peace Through Adversity

The road to Bethlehem is not the romanticized little journey we've come to know from pageants and television. The road to Bethlehem is hard, but at its end lies the fulfillment of the promise of God. Through the years, we've lost sight of what it must have been like for Mary and Joseph in the days leading up to the birth of Jesus. Mary, nine months pregnant, made the 75-mile trip from Nazareth to Bethlehem on the bony back of a donkey. Sustaining her through cold nights, hardship, and the fear of an uncertain future was the knowledge of a promise from God: "And behold, you will bear a son, and you shall name Him Jesus." It's no different for you and me today. When hard times come, nothing will carry you through like a knowledge of God's great promises.

What is your anchor in the middle of difficulty?

*For with God nothing shall be impossible.* (Luke 1:37 KJV)

**Your Gift to Him**

Let me test your knowledge of the Christmas story this morning. According to the Bible, how many wise men followed a star to Bethlehem? Many people will answer "three." After all, doesn't the old Christmas carol say, "We three kings of Orient are...?" Actually, the Bible doesn't say how many wise men came to worship the infant King of kings. It says only that they brought three types of gifts—gold, frankincense, and myrrh—laid them at the feet of Jesus, and worshiped Him. This Christmas, each of us, in our own way, will have the opportunity to do the same thing, but instead of gold, you can give Him something much more precious. You can give Him your life. Nothing you can do will bring you more "peace on earth."

## Are you willing to lay your life down before the Lord?

*And when they were come into the house, they saw the young child with Mary his mother, and fell down, and worshipped him: and when they had opened their treasures, they presented unto him gifts; gold, and frankincense and myrrh.* (Matthew 2:11 KJV)

December

 **Merry Christmas!**

In our familiarity with today's celebrations, it's easy to overlook the fundamental truth behind the Christmas story: God keeps His promises. When Jesus came as a baby, He fulfilled a promise made to the first woman: "Your seed shall crush the serpent's head." He also fulfilled scores of Old Testament prophecies including this one delivered by Isaiah more than 700 years earlier: "For unto us a child is born, and his name shall be called Wonderful Counselor, the mighty God, the Prince of Peace." One more promise that Christmas fulfills is found in the book of John: "For God so loved the world, that He gave His only begotten Son, that whoever believes in Him should not perish, but have eternal life." That's the real story of Christmas—a loving God, keeping His promises.

*Now all this was done, that it might be fulfilled which was spoken of the Lord by the prophet, saying, Behold, a virgin shall be with child, and shall bring forth a son, and they shall call his name Emmanuel, which being interpreted is, God with us.* (Matthew 1:22–23 KJV)

Aren't you glad God keeps His promises?

Image • Brandon Cormier

# Who Is Jesus?

Today we're all in that mopping-up operation called The Day After Christmas. Before we put Christmas completely behind us, permit me some final observations about the holiday. When the Son of God was born, it was not in a plush palace but in a cave. He was laid, not in a crib of gold, but in an animal's feed trough. It may seem odd to us that God chose to present His Son to the world in such an unassuming way, until you begin to understand Jesus' mission. Philippians tells us the Son of God "took the form of a humble servant, being born in human likeness." But the next time He comes to earth, He'll have the fanfare, glory, and majesty befitting a returning King.

## What do you see Jesus as?

*For to us a child is born, to us a son is given, and the government will be on his shoulders. And he will be called Wonderful Counselor, Mighty God, Everlasting Father, Prince of Peace.* (Isaiah 9:6 NIV)

# 27 Salt and Light

Most people tend to be shaped and molded by those around them. A small minority, however, are influencers. Instead of being pulled down to the common average, they lift those around them up to higher levels. If you want to position yourself for a promotion, consider your ability to influence others. Management expert Kenneth Blanchard has written, "The key to successful leadership today is influence, not authority." Jesus talked about the need to influence others in terms of being "salt and light." Purpose to be a person of positive influence. Promotion is sure to follow.

## Are you being influenced by others or influencing them?

*You are the salt of the earth. But if the salt loses its saltiness, how can it be made salty again? ... You are the light of the world. A town built on a hill cannot be hidden* (Matthew 5:13–15 KJV)

#  Keep Going

When people think of Michael Jordan, they think of someone who was the best in his career. What they don't remember is that he missed more than 9,000 shots, lost almost 300 games, and missed game-winning shots twenty-six times. He stated, "I've failed over and over and over again in my life. And that is why I succeed." You are no different than Michael. You will stumble on your way to success. The question is, will you get back up again? The next time you try may be the success you've been looking for. On the other hand, if you stay down, you will never reach the finish line. Don't let the mistakes in your life stop you from pursuing the dream in your heart. Remember, if you don't quit, you will win.

## Have you stopped going forward in some area of your life?

*Fight the good fight of the faith. Take hold of the eternal life to which you were called and about which you made the good confession in the presence of many witnesses.* (1 Timothy 6:12 ESV)

## Pursue Your Dreams

In 1876, a Western Union internal memo stated, "This 'telephone' has too many shortcomings to be seriously considered as a means of communication. The device is inherently of no value to us." Obviously, this assessment has been proven quite wrong. I think it serves as a reminder that you'll always have people who disagree with your ideas, but that doesn't mean you should quit. As Winston Churchill stated, if you want to be successful, never, ever, ever give up. People's opinions are important and can provide valuable input in our lives. That doesn't mean they will understand every idea you have. Don't allow men's opinions to rule your life. Choose to pursue the dream in your heart.

Is there someone in your life who has been holding you back from pursuing your dreams?

*Be ye strong therefore, and let not your hands be weak: for your work shall be rewarded.* (2 Chronicles 15:7 KJV)

#  Love Through Your Communication

Many people unintentionally alienate themselves from others because they don't know how to hold a conversation. When talking with others, they talk about themselves to such an extent that they ignore other people. They may be looking at them and expecting a response, but they have forgotten the golden rule of conversation: actively engage with and be genuinely interested in the people you are talking to. That means stop talking about yourself and think of questions that will allow others to talk about their hobbies, likes, dislikes, and so on. Whether you're talking to close friends or acquaintances, directing conversations toward others will help you win in relationships every time.

Do you show your love for others by putting them first in your conversations?

*Love the Lord your God with all your heart and with all your soul and with all your strength and with all your mind'; and, 'Love your neighbor as yourself"* (Luke 10:27 NIV)

## 31 Vision Propels Your Future

An Austrian psychologist who survived the Nazi camps of World War II made a significant discovery. While imprisoned, he became intrigued with the question of what made it possible for a few people to survive when most died. He found that the common denominator among survivors was not health, vitality, intelligence, or survival skills. The single most important factor in survival was a future-oriented vision—a sense of purpose or mission that compelled them to live. The same is true for us today. Great achievement comes in finding a God-given vision and pursuing it with all your heart. Heading into next year, let God inspire a bold vision for your future, then get started making it a reality.

Have you considered the vision in life God has for you?

*If people can't see what God is doing, they stumble all over themselves; but when they attend to what he reveals, they are most blessed.* (Proverbs 29:18 Msg.)

# Bibliography

1. Edward C. Goodman, The Forbes Book of Business Quotations: 14,266 Thoughts on the Business of Life, Konemann V., 1997.

2. George Sweeting, Who Said That?, Moody Publishers, 1995.

3. Glenn Van Ekeren, Speaker's Sourcebook II: Quotes, Stories, and Anecdotes for Every Occasion, Prentice Hall Press, 2002.

4. Lawrence Kimbrough, Words to Die For: Verses That Shaped the Lives of 30 People Who Changed the World, Holman Reference, 2002.

5. https://quoteinvestigator.com/2016/02/09/boldness/ (January 4).

6. https://allauthor.com/quotes/2273/ (January 9).

7. https://www.goodreads.com/quotes/7145802-you-are-valuable-because-you-exist-not-because-of-what (February 3).

8. https://www.bostonmagazine.com/news/2014/07/29/fomo-history/, Ben Schreckinger, "The Home of FOMO," Boston Magazine (February 4).

9. https://www.quotemaster.org/q5a5dc638317d38b-9cca952f64e0cd8ab, https://www.goodreads.com/quotes/746012-today-not-starting-is-far-far-worse-than-being-wrong (February 10).

10. Mark 9:23, https://www.coolidgefoundation.org/quote/quotations-a/#:~:text=Faith%20is%20the%20great%20motive,part%20of%20an%20un-ending%20plan.%E2%80%9D (February 11).11. Romans 12:3, https://www.forbes.com/quotes/10115/ (February 15).

12. http://blogs.umb.edu/quoteunquote/2012/05/08/its-a-much-more-effective-quotation-to-attribute-it-to-aristotle-rather-than-to-will-durant/ (February 16).

13. https://www.foxnews.com/entertainment/long-lost-dr-seuss-book-published-25-years-after-his-death, https://www.goodreads.com/quotes/185059-i-do-not-think-there-is-any-other-quality-so (February 18).

14. https://www.reaganfoundation.org/ronald-reagan/the-presidency/reagan-the-man/#:~:text=On%20his%20desk%20in%20the,that%20in%20every-thing%20he%20did.&text=That%2C%20more%20than%20anything%20else,the%20Presidency%20of%20Ronald%20Reagan, (February 21).

15. Brian Houston, Twitter account @BrianCHouston, June 22, 2018 (February 22). ·

16. Proverbs 17:9 (February 26).

17. P. Berner, R. Wolf, Psychiatry the State of the Art Volume 4: Psychiatry and Psychosomatic Medicine, Springer, 2012 (March 3).

18. https://www.goodreads.com/quotes/467754-for-marriage-is-like-life-in-this-that-it-is-a (March 5).

19. https://en.wikipedia.org/wiki/The_Four_Loves (March 19).

20. Genesis 1:26–28 (March 21).

21. https://web.cs.dal.ca/~johnston/poetry/island.html (March 26).

22. https://www.brainyquote.com/quotes/thomas_a_edison_132683, https://www.brainyquote.com/quotes/harriet_beecher_stowe_126390 (March 27).

23. http://www.finestquotes.com/quote-id-45755.htm (April 8).

24. Matthew 11:15, Revelation 2:29 (April 9).

25. Proverbs 10:4 (April 14).

26. https://www.brainyquote.com/quotes/william_james_104186 (April 21).

27. Luke 6:38 (April 25).

28. Mark 9:23 (April 28).

29. https://www.goodreads.com/quotes/1216350-every-thing-you-ve-ever-wanted-is-on-the-other-side-of (May 4).

30. https://www.brainyquote.com/quotes/benjamin_franklin_382924, https://www.brainyquote.com/quotes/mark_twain_120156 (May 8).

31. 1 Corinthians 13:5 (May 14).

32. https://www.goodreads.com/quotes/20907-any-fool-can-criticize-complain-and-condemn-and-most-fools-do (May 15).

33. https://www.goodreads.com/quotes/166122-to-for-give-is-to-set-a-prisoner-free-and-discover (May 22).

34. Habakkuk 2:2–3 (May 23).

35. https://www.forbes.com/quotes/3439/ (May 28).

36. https://effectiveedge.com/2016/06/when-the-eyes-say-one-thing-and-the-tongue-another-a-practiced-man-relies-on-the-language-of-the-first-ralph-waldo-emerson/#:~:text=%22When%20the%20eyes%20say%20one,Ralph%20Waldo%20Emerson%20%2D%20Effective%20Edge (June 5).

37. Ephesians 4:23, Galatians 6:9 (June 11).

38. Ecclesiastes 4:9–11 (June 13).

39. https://www.brainyquote.com/quotes/aeschy-lus_148572 (June 27).

40. Proverbs 22:29 (July 3).

41. https://en.wikipedia.org/wiki/First_inauguration_of_Franklin_D._Roosevelt, https://www.goodreads.com/quotes/3823-you-gain-strength-courage-and-confidence-by-every-experience-in (July 7).

42. Matthew 5:41 (July 8).

43. https://www.goodreads.com/quotes/617982-the-world-we-d-discovered-doesn-t-love-you-like-your-family (July 11).

44. https://www.goodreads.com/quotes/812245-you-are-never-too-old-to-set-another-goal-or (July 15).

45. Proverbs 16:13 (July 18).

46. https://www.goodreads.com/quotes/2749-nothing-in-this-world-can-take-the-place-of-persistence (July 21).

47. https://www.azquotes.com/quote/859845 (July 22).

48. https://www.brainyquote.com/quotes/abraham_lin-coln_151229 (July 23).

49. https://www.goodreads.com/quotes/37169-cour-age-is-not-simply-one-of-the-virtues-but-the, https://www.brainyquote.com/quotes/thomas_jeffer-son_120901 (July 25).

50. https://www.azquotes.com/quote/877828 (August 6).

51. https://www.brainyquote.com/quotes/washington_ir-ving_122774, Proverbs 20:3 (August 8).

52. https://www.goodreads.com/quotes/7288468-hu-mility-is-not-thinking-less-of-yourself-it-s-thinking-of (August 12).

53. https://www.presidency.ucsb.edu/documents/me-morial-day-address-arlington-national-cemetery-1 (August 14–15).

54. https://www.brainyquote.com/quotes/benjamin_franklin_151645 (August 16).

55. https://www.goodreads.com/quotes/118854-com-ing-together-is-the-beginning-keeping-together-is-progress-working, https://www.goodreads.com/quotes/745249-unity-has-never-meant-uniformity (August 17).

56. https://www.goodreads.com/quotes/201557-what-seems-to-us-as-bitter-trials-are-often-blessings (August 18).

57. https://www.brainyquote.com/quotes/saint_fran-cis_de_sales_193305 (August 19).

58. https://www.brainyquote.com/quotes/helen_keller_382259 (August 20).

59. https://www.brainyquote.com/quotes/theodore_roosevelt_122116 (August 23).

60. https://www.positivelypositive.com/quotes/true-forgiveness-is-not-an-action-after-the-fact-it-is-an-attitude-with-which-you-enter-each-moment/ (August 26).

61. https://www.brainyquote.com/quotes/mark_twain_100358, https://www.brainyquote.com/quotes/henry_david_thoreau_132515#:~:text=Henry%20David%20Thoreau%20Quotes&text=The%20greatest%20compliment%20that%20was%20ever%20paid%20me%20was%20when,and%20attended%20to%20my%20answer (August 27).

62. https://www.brainyquote.com/quotes/norman_vincent_peale_130593 (August 30).

63. https://www.brainyquote.com/quotes/albert_einstein_130625 (August 31).

64. https://www.goodreads.com/quotes/706001-resorting-to-lying-or-cheating-in-any-competition-amounts-to (September 3).

65. https://www.goodreads.com/quotes/311976-faith-does-not-eliminate-questions-but-faith-knows-where-to (September 4).

66. https://www.brainyquote.com/quotes/albert_einstein_121993 (September 5).

67. https://www.forbes.com/quotes/76/ (September 7).

68. https://quotefancy.com/quote/1310938/Peyton-Manning-If-you-work-hard-and-you-play-well-all-those-critics-quiet-themselves (September 8).

69. https://www.goodreads.com/quotes/457416-when-you-re-good-at-something-you-ll-tell-everyone-when-you-re, Proverbs 18:16 (September 9).

70. https://www.goodreads.com/quotes/5156-i-learned-that-courage-was-not-the-absence-of-fear (September 11).

71. https://quotefancy.com/quote/1129685/Gary-Chapman-Conflicts-are-not-a-sign-you-ve-married-the-wrong-person-They-simply-affirm (September 13).

72. https://www.brainyquote.com/quotes/emmitt_smith_481818 (September 14).

73. https://quotefancy.com/quote/1103211/Tom-Brady-I-don-t-care-about-three-years-ago-I-don-t-care-about-two-years-ago-I-don-t (September 15).

74. https://www.goodreads.com/quotes/389221-never-say-never-because-limits-like-fears-are-often-just (September 16).

75. https://www.forbes.com/quotes/8996/ (September 18).

76. https://thegolfnewsnet.com/golfnewsnetteam/2015/03/31/rory-mcilroy-letter-tiger-woods-im-coming-for-you-10492/ (September 19).

77. https://www.brainyquote.com/quotes/wade_boggs_311616 (September 21).

78. https://www.goodreads.com/quotes/709847-learning-is-the-only-thing-the-mind-never-exhausts-never (September 22).

79. https://www.goodreads.com/quotes/14109-faith-is-not-the-belief-that-god-will-do-what (September 25).

80. https://www.brainyquote.com/quotes/doug_larson_107911 (September 27).

81. 1 Corinthians 14:9 (October 2).

82. Matthew 12:25, Amos 3:3 (October 4).

83. https://www.brainyquote.com/quotes/zig_ziglar_125675 (October 9).

84. https://www.goodreads.com/quotes/66756-he-that-speaks-much-is-much-mistaken (October 20).

85. https://www.brainyquote.com/quotes/henry_win-kler_320340 (October 26).

86. Proverbs 28:20 (October 27).

87. https://quotefancy.com/quote/780711/C-S-Lewis-Selfishness-has-never-been-admired (October 31).

88. http://www.foundingfatherquotes.com/quote/962 (November 1).

89. Proverbs 3:14–18 (November 2).

90. Psalm 139:23-24 (November 9).

91. https://www.goodreads.com/quotes/4072403-with-integrity-you-have-nothing-to-fear-since-you-have (November 10).

92. https://www.brainyquote.com/quotes/ralph_wal-do_emerson_101478 (November 12).

93. https://www.brainyquote.com/quotes/carl_sand-burg_121791 (November 16).

94. https://underthebluedoor.org/2014/01/23/gratitude-like-faith-is-a-muscle-the-more-you-use-it-the-stronger-it-grows-and-the-more-pow-er-you-have-to-use-it-on-your-behalf-if-you-do-not-practice-gratefulness-its-benefaction-will-go-unn/ (November 20).

95. Jon Acuff, Twitter account @jonacuff, 2020 (November 28). ·

96. https://www.brainyquote.com/quotes/carl_lew-is_395507, https://www.passiton.com/inspirational-quotes/6512-you-can-t-put-a-limit-on-anything-the-more-you (December 4).

97. https://www.goodreads.com/quotes/194078-the-thing-i-hate-about-an-argument-is-that-it (December 7).

98. https://www.dailymail.co.uk/news/article-2325853/Jeremy-Affelft-Baseball-player-overpaid-500K-re-turns-cash-San-Francisco-Giants.html (December 10).

99. https://www.google.com/search?q=dictio-nary+peace&rlz=1C1CHBF_enUS878US878&oq=dic-tionary+peace&aqs=chrome..69i57j0j0i22i30l6.254 0j0j4&sourceid=chrome&ie=UTF-8 (December 11).

100. https://www.goodreads.com/quotes/648005-not-much-happens-without-a-dream-and-for-something-great (December 12).

101. https://www.goodreads.com/author/quotes/5139. Charles_R_Swindoll (December 13).

102. https://www.goodreads.com/quotes/519851-there-is-no-limit-to-what-can-be-accomplished-if (December 14).

103. Proverbs 10:19 (December 18).

104. Isaiah 7:14 (December 21).

105. Luke 1:31 (December 23).

106. Isaiah 9:6 (December 25).

107. Philippians 2:7 (December 26).

108. https://www.forbes.com/quotes/11194/ (December 28).

109. https://www.pbs.org/wgbh/nova/time/through2.html (December 29).